Dundee Memories

Ian M. Malcolm

Birlinn

IN ASSOCIATION WITH
THE EUROPEAN ETHNOLOGICAL RESEARCH CENTRE
THE NATIONAL MUSEUMS OF SCOTLAND

Flashbacks

The Flashback series is sponsored by the European Ethnological Research
Centre, c/o the National Museums of Scotland, Chambers Street,
Edinburgh EH1 1JF
General Editor: Alexander Fenton

Other titles in the Flashback series include

Contents

First published in 2005 by
Birlinn Limited
West Newington House
10 Newington Road
Edinburgh EH9 1QS

www.birlinn.co.uk

ISBN10: 1 84158 406 1
ISBN13: 978 1 84158 406 5

British Library Cataloguing-in-Publication Data
A catalogue record for this book is available from the
British Library

The publisher acknowledges subsidy from the Scottish Inheritance Fund
towards the publication of this book.

Typeset by Wordsense Ltd, Edinburgh
Printed and bound by Nørhaven Paperback A/S, Viborg

1 Blackness Road

I was born in a farm worker's cottage by the side of the Dichty Burn, at Douglasfield, by Dundee, in the District of Broughty Ferry, on 27 April 1925. My maternal grandfather was a ploughman, and the cottage stood at the northern boundary of what is now the large housing estate of Douglas. But my parents obtained a house in the tenement at 219 Blackness Road, Dundee, so that my first and subsequent memories centre round that place, which was home to me until I left Dundee in 1953.

Number 219 Blackness Road, or Thorn Place as it was once known, is the first of a row of tenements which stretch from Glenagnes Road* to Ashbank. All have balconies, which we called 'plats' (perhaps an abbreviation of platform). The tenements continue to be occupied, but, when the town council acquired them from private ownership in the 1960s, they turned two houses into one and installed bathrooms so that today's occupants enjoy a much higher standard of living than we did.

Until at least the 1970s, 219 Blackness Road was easily identified by the posters which always adorned its windowless east wall. Our house was on the top or third storey, with only another house between it and the

---

* Often referred to as the Hennie Roadie as this had been its name when only a earthen path.

end house of the next tenement. We overlooked Logie Housing Scheme and had wonderful views of the Law, the fields on which Pentland Housing Scheme now stands, and Balgay Hill. Incidentally, although Logie Housing (Corporation) Scheme was built at the end of the First World War to accommodate the returning servicemen, the rents were so high that the majority, which included my father and at least four others in the land (tenement), could not afford them. Some people may look down on council housing today, but we looked up to those who lived in Logie. In this regard, however, our next-door neighbour on the western side must have been the exception as, unlike everyone else we knew, his weekly wage apparently brought him into the income tax bracket.

Nobody ever referred to a tenement house as a 'flat'. Our house consisted of only a small lobby, in which stood a chest of drawers, and two rectangular rooms laid end to end. The front room, with its window on the plat, was called the kitchen although it was also the sitting room and my parents' bedroom. The other room, which served as a second bedroom, was the posh one where visitors might be entertained on special occasions, and its window overlooked Blackness Road. The house was in fact a 'but and ben', and when something was in the back room we referred to it as being 'ben the room'.

At the window in the kitchen was a wooden bunker into which the coalman deposited the weekly delivery of 'chirls', the small coal which my mother preferred, and the lid of the bunker served as a work surface. Beside the bunker was the sink where all personal and dish washing was done. As the tap emitted only cold water, water was heated on either the gas cooker or the coal fire. To begin with, there was a 'range', but, after a 'modern' fire was installed, there was, during cold weather, always a black cast-iron kettle on one of the hobs which swung over the fire and provided hot water. A gas cooker stood close to the sink and a press/cupboard, for dishes etc. was in the wall to the right of it. Fixed to the ceiling was the indispensable pulley.

The furniture in the kitchen consisted of my parents' bed, a couch and a few dining room chairs. When my mother was at ease, she sat in a rocking chair on solid supports, which had been her mother's. My father had an upright wooden chair with arms. It always had newspapers or magazines under the cushion and nobody else ever sat there when he was in the house. The only other furniture was a dressing table with an oval mirror. After the installation of an inside lavatory, my parents' bed was hemmed in on three sides. This made it difficult to make the bed, and, as it was impossible to reach to the back from a standing position, a stick was kept to smooth out the covers.

'Ben the room' there was a greyish three-piece suite, which had apparently been bought second-hand, a double bed, a large dresser and a pedal organ. Although my mother was musical, with a fine singing

voice, and had had a few lessons when young, I was the only one who took pleasure in using the organ.*
A black cast-iron gas fire, in a grate and surrounded, as the kitchen fire was, by a fender, was available to provide heat. But, as money was at a premium, it was lit only on special occasions. Between the fire and the window, with the required aspidistra on a carved Indian table with a decorated brass** top, was a press which contained books on all subjects. My father was a largely self-taught scholar, and it was always a sore point with my mother that she was denied use of the press. The only other storage space available was under the beds.

The floor covering was wax cloth (linoleum) with rugs placed in front of the fires and, until electricity was installed at the tenant's expense, lighting was provided by gas mantles in both rooms. Dust was removed from the rugs, by hanging them over a washing line in the back green and beating them hard with a cane carpet beater.

Up to the first two landings of the tenement, the stairs were under cover, with their walls 'decorated' with a dirty-looking brown ochre which marked your clothing if you came against them. After the second landing, the stairs emerged into the open, and the lavatory which

---

* When the organ was disposed of in the late 1940s, half-a-crown (2s 6d/12½p) had to be paid to have it taken away!
** Brasso was used to polish this and other objects requiring such treatment.

stood near the top of them served the families in the four houses on the top storey. The occupants of the houses on the lower levels were similarly provided for, and this, I was told, was an improvement on the communal lavatory which had stood in the back green when the tenement was built. A gas lamp, located by the stairs at each level, provided light for landings and stairs, and this remained the case even after all the houses had electricity. Apart from Blackness Road, the adjoining streets had gas lamps, and the 'leerie' who lit them, by means of a light on a long pole, was a familiar sight. In the early 1930s, each house was provided with an inside lavatory – the space for it being taken from the kitchen.

My paternal grandparents lived at the east end of the landing beneath us. On 5 May 1929, I was playing in their house when my father came in saying that he had a present for me and asked me to guess what it was. My guesses, which included 'A cake?', were well wide of the mark. I had a baby brother. Nobody had their babies in hospital in those days and, even in the limited space of these tenement houses, there were families with three children of mixed sex. Incidentally, Miss Janie Macintosh, who lived alone on the second landing, was well known in the district because she continued, right up to her death in the 1950s, to wear the clothes of the Victorian era.

Immediately behind the tenement was an earthen area known as the 'backs' or 'backies'. This, together with the large communal 'green' from which it was separated by a fence, was our play area. Every family had a cellar in the backies – the cellars at the eastern end being under the walkway, between the inner end of the uncovered close and the stairs, and those at the western end built against the tenement wall. This meant that we could climb on to the latter, but, as this put us on a level with the rear windows of the two ground-floor houses and the roof was made of corrugated iron, old Mrs McKinnes and her son, Arthur, would rage at us from their window.

Washing was done in the communal washhouse at the entrance to the green. A fire had to be lit in the boiler to provide hot water. Washing was dried on the green, and each family had their day of using the wooden poles. The mangle in the washhouse was owned by Miss Dolan. She charged nothing for its use, but my mother always gave her a present at Christmas. During inclement weather, washing was dried on the pulley in the kitchen where, in any case, it was hung to 'air'.

Persuaded by my father, my mother and grandmother eventually took advantage of the facilities provided at Logie Washhouse. They soon found it a boon, and it was a common sight to see women pushing prams, laden with baskets of clothes, heading to and from corporation washhouses. The steamies, as they were known, were places where women socialized, and I think my mother missed this when she eventually moved to a brand new corporation house and got a washing machine. Due to the proliferation of such machines, Logie Washhouse was eventually closed on 17 February 1973, after providing fifty years' service to the community.

Alice Durie, who lived on the landing below and was four months older than I, was my first playmate. There was a hole in the fence which separated the 'green' from Glenagnes Street and I clearly remember that, when I made to enter the space first, she, although only four, admonished me by saying 'It's ladies before gentlemen.' My mother, whom I addressed as Mammy, was on the plat watching us, so I bawled out to her for confirmation of this etiquette rule. A row of garages now lines Glenagnes Street by the side of this fence.

The only pets we ever had were a goldfish and a newt. The goldfish survived for many years, but the newt, acquired from the water in the disused Hillside Quarry, located somewhere in the Menzies Hill area, had a short life. Hillside Quarry, with its high sides, was a place my mother didn't like us going to, but the only occasion when something happened was when my father and grandfather went with us and my father fell into shallow water!

2 Blackness Public School – 'The Blackie'

Some parents have a problem in taking their children to school for the first time, but this was not one which my parents experienced as I prigged with my mother to take me when Alice went and I was left without a playmate. I was still only four, therefore, when my mother took me down to Blackness Public School, immediately west of Forest Park Road, and we entered the infants' class taken by Miss Findlay. Miss Findlay asked me if I knew anyone in the class and, when I said 'Alice', she told me to go and sit beside her. The class was drawing figures in trays of sand at the time, but, as Alice was shortly moved up a class, we did not go through school together.

I have to thank Miss Findlay for a good start to my education. I remember her for two specific reasons. One day, when she asked if anyone could recite any poetry, I stood up and gave the following rendering of 'The Boy Stood On The Burning Deck', which my grandfather had taught me.

> The boy stood on the burning deck,
> His feet were rade (red) wi' blisters.
> He got the sark burned aff his back
> And had tae wear his sister's.

I was asked to repeat the word 'sark' (shirt) and, although Miss Findlay made no adverse comment, my effort must have caused hilarity in the staffroom, if there was one. The second incident regarding Miss Findlay was when I met her as I was coming out of the Wireless College in Windsor Street in the spring of 1943. I had never seen her since leaving Blackness School yet she greeted me by name.

The reason that I am not sure if there was a staff-room is that teachers boiled water for their morning tea by connecting the lead of an electric kettle into the suspended light socket above their desks. When playtime was over, water to wash the dishes was boiled in the same way, and a pupil helped to dry them.

As I moved up the school, I had Miss Thom, Miss Swan, Mr Brown and Mr Mackenzie. There were no married women teachers, as women had to leave the profession when they married. All head teachers were men. This was, of course, wrong in both respects, but the pendulum has swung too far the other way concerning the latter. Almost all primary head teachers are now women, and there is an imbalance with too few men in primary schools.

The headmaster was a tall severe man called Mr Jack, and the only time I had any dealings with him was when I was called to his room, accused of tearing another boy's winter coat in the playground. I had nothing to do with it, but the boy had reported to his mother that I had done it and she complained to Mr Jack. I was about eight at the time and, of course, professed my innocence, but Mr Jack would have none of it and browbeat me so much that I burst into tears and 'confessed' to a crime I had not committed. That was the last I heard of the incident, and I made no mention of it to my parents.

As Miss Swan lived in Logie, she knew my mother and they often conversed. All the teachers seemed to play the piano, and Miss Swan tested our hearing skill by playing groups of four notes which we had to identify by the sol-fa method. I usually got them right and one day, when I was playing the mouth organ as I walked home from school, Miss Swan caught up with me and said, 'Now I know how you recognise the notes.' The old Scottish songs were part of our education, and rightly so, yet my own children went through primary school thirty years later without being taught them.

Mr Brown took the football team, and every week we had to remain after school to see who had been selected. On one occasion, when he went out of the room, a boy peed in the inkwells* and, as there was a mess on the desks and floor, Mr Brown was furious. I cannot recollect if the boy was caught, but none of us thought his behaviour the least bit funny.

---

* The ink, of inferior quality, was kept in a bottle of about the same size and shape as the average whisky bottle with a narrow metal dispenser at the top to allow access to the hole in the inkwell. The pens, provided by the school, had a wooden stem with a metal piece into which the nib was inserted. The ballpoint pen, at first very expensive, arrived towards the end of the Second World War, but the older method was still used in schools into the 1960s. In consequence, blotting paper was necessary to soak up surplus ink.

In winter, Mr Brown and his girlfriend took about half-a-dozen members of the class to a cinema on Saturday afternoons. The names were drawn from a bowler hat, and I was delighted when mine was amongst them. We were taken to see *Clive of India* at the King's Theatre in the Cowgate, and when I offered the money my parents had given me, it was refused.

Many teachers involved themselves in unpaid extra-curricular activities, but this ceased in the 1980s due to the overbearing attitudes of local authorities. I have a notion that Mr Brown became head of another primary school.

The Silver Jubilee of King George V and Queen Mary occurred in 1935, when I was ten, and I still have the now-battered tin chocolate box, suitably inscribed and decorated with their portraits, which we were all given. On another occasion, when the Duke and Duchess of York (later George VI and Queen Elizabeth) visited Dundee, we were provided with small Union Jacks and taken to Blackness Avenue by our teachers to wave them at the royal car as it whizzed past us. At the time of the Duke of Windsor's romance with Mrs Wallis Simpson and his subsequent abdication from the throne, a joke which went the rounds was 'Why did the Duke of Windsor knock three times at Mrs Simpson's door?' To which the answer was 'Because there were twa chaps afore him!'

To my mind, it was a criminal act when teachers were forbidden to teach grammar. No one can understand English without a knowledge of grammar, and it becomes imperative when learning a foreign language. Mr Mackenzie, who took primary 7 and subsequently became headmaster, taught us parsing and, with a book in front of us, we had to take turns in stating whether the word was a noun, verb, etc. As the questions went round the class from pupil to pupil, we anxiously counted ahead to see which word we would have to parse. I was always a bit of a dreamer, and one day, when Mr Mackenzie noticed my lack of attention, he called out to me saying, 'Baa, baa black sheep – what colour were the sheep?' Roused from my reverie, I answered 'White'!

Girls from the Balgay Industrial School, on Blackness Road just west of Kelso Street, attended the school and were easily identified as they wore a brown uniform with a peculiar box-shaped hat. The rest of us wore no uniform, and I don't remember any of these girls moving on to Logie Central School. At primary school, we all carried our books in leather school bags (satchels), worn on our backs like rucksacks.

Disagreements between boys were normally settled after school. And when the cry 'Fight' went up, a crowd followed the combatants into the small cul-de-sac of nearby Rosefield Place where the issue was to be settled. On the occasion when I was involved, I landed a beauty at the outset, but, largely due to the fact that the protectors in my shoes caused me to keep slipping on the road, I was soundly defeated.

In true brotherly fashion, I was giving Eric a hammering on the way to school one day and, witnessing the unequal contest, a man intervened. But Eric immediately piped up and said, 'It's all right, he's my brother!'

Fife was ahead of Dundee in selecting pupils to go on to a senior secondary school. In Dundee, only a chosen few, selected by the teacher of Primary 7, sat the bursary exam and, if they passed, went to Harris or Morgan Academies. This meant that almost all working-class children were transferred from their primary schools to Logie Central School, Rockwell or Stobswell, although many were brighter than their counterparts at the academies who were there only because their parents paid fees.

I have no recollection of sitting a qualifying exam, but remember undergoing a test with a few others. And, when I was put into the commercial class at Logie, but denied French, I came in later years to believe that I was a borderline pupil for the French section. This exclusion from French caused me considerable distress when I went to Logie – and scientists will find it of interest that their subject was considered to be the easier alternative!

The less academic boys and girls were placed into technical and domestic science classes respectively, and the whole arrangement was geared to providing suitable labour for industry. The more academic boys became clerks, and the more academic girls worked as typists (typing was not available to boys) and shorthand typists. The less academic boys turned into tradesmen and labourers, while the girls in the same category became shop assistants, labourers and housewives. Yet, although the system worked well for industry, it left the so-called brighter boy handicapped when attempting any do-it-yourself job in the home.

Blackness School closed in 1981 and was demolished. Flats were built on the site, but its name was transferred to the Hawkhill School. Blackness, which had opened in 1888, was the only school which my father had attended. But it was there that a male teacher had taught him Latin roots plus a little shorthand and French. My grandfather had been a half-timer at the Hawkie – working in the morning and attending school in the afternoon.

3 Grandparents

I was fortunate indeed in having my grandparents living so close, as my grandfather never tired of playing with me and I was allowed a freedom in their house that I was denied in my own. As he was fond of repairing clocks, he had a collection of spare parts and I spun the wheels on a bare wooden chair. Under his instruction, I learned how to spin a peerie (top), and he made stilts for me when I was older. Incidentally, he was also a great one for attending to young birds which fell from the trees lining the drive next to the tenement. This was done by masticating bread or oatmeal and feeding a young bird from his mouth.

Grandad was a 'Red Lichtie' (a native of Arbroath), and he and my grandmother took Eric and me on an annual trip to Arbroath. We went by train from the East Station (closed in 1959) and the Elliot Junction rail disaster of 1906 was usually mentioned when the train halted there. On arriving in Arbroath, we might spend some time in the town itself, but our destination was the cliffs.

In those car-less days, we thought nothing of walking all the way to the Mason's Cove, where we picnicked. As we walked along the cliff path, Grandad picked sourocks (sorrel) for us to chew, and we shouted to raise an echo at Dickman's Den. At the cove, Eric and I had a great time playing on the 'flairs', and welks, dulse and limpets were gathered to be brought home, boiled and eaten. Once, when it rained and we took shelter with others in the entrance to the cove itself, Grandad set up a cairn of stones and everyone soon joined in the fun of throwing stones to knock it down.

I was quite small on the only occasion that we visited a relative in Arbroath whose concreted backyard contained a pit in which to turn herring into 'smokies'. My father was with us. Recognising him immediately, the elderly lady, who answered the door, welcomed him with the words 'Come awa' in bye, Jum (Jim).'

Grandad was keen on fishing, and we fished for flooks (flounders) from the sea wall at the Coup* – officially known as Riverside Drive. It was an area on which the city's refuse had been 'couped' or dumped in order to reclaim it from the estuary of the Tay. We fished only with lines, at the end of which were his beautifully plaited leaders. As the best bait was small crabs we called 'piller', we sometimes waded out to the sandbanks to seek them out under stones or discarded tins, when the tide was low.

In his youth, Grandad had been a sportsman. As a swimmer, he had engaged in high diving contests and claimed to have dived off the Tay (railway) Bridge. He had been in the rowing team of Belmont Works, on a site now occupied by Dundee University, and, as wicket-keeper, had captained one of the cricket teams which inaugurated the opening of Lochee Park in 1899. Every year, he took me to the annual Forfarshire v. Perthshire match at Forthill, where he would exchange greetings with Forfarshire's Norman Ireland, who was his great nephew. In August 1938 we went to see Australia v. Scotland. As Don Bradman was in the Australian team, captained by McCabe, the crowds flocked to Forthill.

---

* Before it finally settled on Ingliston as its permanent site, the Royal Highland Show was held annually in each of the four main Scottish cities, and we attended one on the Coup. Fairs, known in Dundee as carnivals, were also held there, and I remember seeing a small red-haired man diving from a great height into a tank of water, risking his life for mere pennies thrown into the tank.

To the disappointment of all, however, Bradman didn't appear and was reputed to have chosen to remain in Edinburgh that day. But it was a great day out and I still have the scorecard with pencilled-in scores in my boyish handwriting. Grandad had little or no interest in football, which he considered to have been ruined when the payment of players was introduced.

Although she appeared more austere than my grandfather, my grandmother was equally indulgent with Eric and me. As she had been 'in service' when young, she knew the right way to do everything in the home. She was a superb cook and baker (everything done on a range which was taken out only after they had died), and I was sometimes given two wooden spatulas to shape the butter into balls. Although I never saw her play the flute, she had been a flautist in the Dundee Ladies' Orchestra, and many an evening was spent singing the old Scot's songs and others such as 'John Peel', 'Molly Malone' and 'I'm Off To Philadelphia In The Morning'. When we made a trip to The Ferry (Broughty Ferry), I was allowed to bring back a bucketful of sand to play with on newspapers laid on the kitchen floor.

My grandparents always had pets: a budgie in the earlier years and then cats. The budgie was seldom in its cage and, instead, would be found walking about on the table or perched on a shoulder while we played games. Cards or games such as tiddlywinks, played on the plain wooden table with a blanket spread to give purchase, were a favourite evening pastime. As for the cat – a friend claimed that 'the very cat flew when Eric entered the house.'

When I was in their house and my father came in, political issues of the day would be discussed and I would hear the names Stanley Baldwin, Ramsey MacDonald, Winston Churchill, Lloyd George, Dingle Foot, Florence Horsburgh and Ned Scrymgeour.* And, naturally, they talked of the recent Great War (First World War), when I learned something of the agony of the trenches, white feathers and rationing. The South African War also came under discussion. I got the idea that their sympathies lay more with the Boers, and they claimed that Joseph Chamberlain had shipped out rifles, concealed in grand pianos. Grandad had joined the Black Watch in 1886 and, with his tendency to exaggerate, he had the pen poised to sign on as a regular when someone advised him to enlist in the militia first to see if he liked the Army. This is what he did – and he left after six months in Perth.

It was with great amusement that my grandparents related an apocryphal story concerning the visit of Queen Victoria and Prince Albert to Dundee in 1844, some twenty-odd years before they were born. According to them, when the Queen stepped ashore

---

* In the General Election of 1922, Edwin Scrymgeour, the Prohibition Party candidate whom my father supported, defeated Churchill and entered Parliament.

from the Royal Yacht, she was so frightened by the fierce-looking mob waiting to welcome her that she promptly returned on board! According to the history books, however, the royal party had a most successful visit, as the queen again did in 1879 when on her way back from Balmoral by train, only months before the Tay Bridge disaster.

I also heard of the crane driver who fell to his death and whose wages were stopped the minute he hit the concrete floor and of my grandmother's younger brother, Jim, who had never been heard of again, after going to Australia.

Although he was never out of Scotland, the stories Grandad told me were often about his adventures in Africa, such as the time when he sat down on a log which moved when he struck a match on it and proved to be a crocodile! But he wasn't joking when he spoke of seeing Ernest Shackleton, of lighting Churchill's cigar and of hearing John McGonagall recite his poems. Like so many others, he treated McGonagall as a joke, and had apparently heard a wag ask the bard if he approved of putting false teeth in the mouth of the Tay.

In all the time I knew them, my grandparents never had a holiday, but I did hear of holidays before and after the Great War spent at the Jubilee Tavern in Burntisland, which was owned by Grandma's sister and her husband, Bob Murray. Dad recounted how he had been almost cut off by the incoming tide at the

Black Rocks and of going on a milk cart on its rounds to the Binn Village. And there was the day when, as a young man, he made an unexpected appearance at the Jubilee, when his parents were staying there, and was greeted by the question 'What aboot Jocky? Did ye gie him water?' Jocky was their pet blackbird, and Dad immediately had to hightail it back home.

4 Fun and Games

Including the four houses on the ground floor whose doors faced directly onto Blackness Road, there were sixteen houses in the land. Although there were no children in seven of these, there was something like twenty-three in the others. This meant that a number of us often played together in the backs or green. We played at skipping, using a long rope and with two or three jumping in the middle while the others sang a jingle such as 'Jelly on the plate, jelly on the plate, wiggle waggle wiggle waggle, jelly on the plate.' Balls could be kicked against the wall separating the backs from the next land. The wall of the washhouse afforded a base for 'keepie-up' at headers, and the poles to which washing ropes were attached became bases for a game involving running between them. When I got thirsty, I would race upstairs to my grandparents' house for a drink – not only was it nearer than my own but I also knew that I would get lemonade there instead of the water generally available in my own! Incidentally, Catholic and non-Catholic children played together. Religion never even entered our minds or, I believe, those of the adults.

Concerning religion, the annual fracas of Saint Patrick's Day had almost disappeared when I was young, but not quite. On that day, gangs of boys, perhaps wearing a small piece of blue or green ribbon and carrying pieces of wood as weapons, would confront other boys with the question 'Scotch or Irish?' (Protestant or Catholic?). And if the answer was not to their liking, they dealt out a hammering. I say the practice had not quite died out because the question was put to me when I was about ten. This was near the top of Glenagnes Road on a dark evening and, although I had only a vague notion of what it was all about and not a clue as to their allegiance, the prospect of a beating-up was all too evident. Fortunately, and greatly to my relief, my answer – 'Scotch' – was the right one. The gang became instantly friendly and I was invited to join in their quest for the Irish.

At first, the 'green' had only grass, but the tenants got together and decided to make a flowered border to improve its look. This, too, eventually afforded some sport for the children as matchboxes were placed on the tops of the canes which supported the taller flowers to capture forkies/forkie-tailies (earwigs), and we took delight in disposing of their destructive occupants. As horse-drawn carts were common in the streets, horse droppings were collected for manure.

Many of the men in the area worked at Blackness Foundry and they provided boys with small polished pieces of steel for the game of pinner, which was generally played against school pals for cigarette cards. The object of the game was to hit the other fellow's pinner from any distance within range. Opponents took turnabout and, when you made a successful strike, you collected. Another unofficial product produced for us at Blackness Foundry was steel girds (hoops), together with the cleeks with which they were propelled. Incidentally, although Blackness Foundry closed down some forty years ago, the building was demolished only in 2000 to make the site available for the houses which now stand there.

A piler – known as a bogey in Edinburgh, a guidy in Glasgow and a tracy in Lanarkshire – was another source of fun. This was a four-wheeled wooden box with the two front wheels on a pivoting axle, secured under a projecting crosspiece at the front to allow guiding (steering). Many pilers had no brakes, and, although pram wheels made for a faster and more comfortable ride, my piler had at first only solid wooden wheels with a primitive handbrake on the right rear wheel. Glenagnes Street made an excellent piler run, as it did a sledge run in winter.

Played with buttons, 'mites' was another popular game. With your arm bent back into a horizontal position, a number of buttons was placed along it. You whipped your arm down in an attempt to catch as many as you could, and any that you missed were then placed on your opponent's arm. Alternatively, mites would be thrown to see who could get one nearest to a wall, and the player who succeeded collected the lot. When it rained, we would acquire a flat piece of rubber, cut it into a round shape and attached a length of string to its centre. Placed on a wet surface, it was impossible to dislodge it with a straightforward pull. If hide and seek were played, we would run up the stairs, climb over the railings and slide back down the metal poles, which supported the plats, to ground level. My mother would have had a fit if she'd known. In autumn, Balgay Hill was a source for chestnuts, which were threaded on string. Selecting the first one on the string, you whacked it against your opponent's, which, if it broke, meant that your own chestnut became a once-er and then a twos-er, etc. as your nut survived.

We never went in for vandalism of any kind. If we had done and were discovered, our parents would soon have made certain that it was not repeated. Regarding punishment, my parents generally applied sanctions, but the leather strap on which my father sharpened his open razor could be put to another use if necessary! We were guilty, however, of plundering apple and pear trees and collecting all the doormats in a tenement, placing them in a heap at a bottom door in the close, before knocking at the door and running.

A great source of entertainment was helping Andra Lamont, who, with his wife and grown-up daughter, Doris, lived in the detached house to the east of the tenement. Andra ran a milk delivery service from the stone-flagged dairy at the back of his house, and we would gather there for the evening delivery when the help we gave was stoking the fire and then delivering the milk. Most of Andra's customers lived in Logie, but, although some lived as far west as Glamis Road, all deliveries were made 'on foot'. People left jugs on their doorsteps, and we filled them from the metal flagons we carried. At the end of the evening, payment was made in the dairy. If we were lucky, this would be a penny, but, more often, when Mrs Lamont or Doris were involved, they would descend the stairs from the house to dispense dry tea-bread. Armed with this knowledge and when I would be reluctant to do something in the house, my mother would ridicule me for working for Andra Lamont for an old bap. Although a penny, at least, was welcome, it was secondary to the fun we had in the dairy, as Andra was a tolerant man who let us do what we liked. In those days the driveway between the tenement and Andra's house, which linked Blackness Road to Glenagnes Street, was used as a public thoroughfare, but a subsequent occupier closed it off. Incidentally, Petrie, the coalman, stabled his horse beside the dairy.

Another Andra in my life was Andra Gracie who sold fruit and vegetables from his horse-driven cart. One day when he was in Glenagnes Street and talking my mother, he mentioned that his boy assistant had not turned up. She said that I would lend a hand if he wanted it, so I soon found myself in the pleasant position of sitting on the slow-moving cart as it proceeded west. We were in the region of Kelso Street and, as Andra was making a delivery, I was alone when a lady approached and asked the price of first one thing and then another. And, as the reply to her questions was 'I don't know', she said 'What good are you?'

While fish could be purchased at a local shop, it was often bought from an Arbroath 'fish wife'. These hardy, itinerant ladies, dressed in black and with a striped apron, arrived in Dundee by train. With their heavily laden baskets carried in front of them by means of a broad band slung over their necks, they trudged their own sectors of the city and climbed the stairs, just as the coalmen had to do, of the innumerable tenements.

In summer, an 'Ingin (Onion) Johnny' would call with strings of onions round his neck. These Breton men and one woman 'Onion Jenny', working from fixed bases in Dundee, Leith, Glasgow, Aberdeen, Ayr and a few other places, sold their onions throughout the country. I seem to remember them using only bicycles to transport their produce, although some apparently still used the earlier long pole, carried on the shoulder.

The 1920s and early 1930s were years of high unemployment. As money was scarce and every penny had to be accounted for, my weekly pocket money was generally a mere hape-ny* (half penny/½d). (This was not, however, the lowest coin as the farthing had that distinction.) Yet pennies, wrapped in paper so that they could be seen, were thrown to beggars who came to sing in the back green, and my mother would invite them to sit in the lobby to have a plate of homemade soup. From time to time, Blind Matty would appear, and we all gathered round to watch her playing the accordion while vigorously stamping her foot. The appearance of a rag-and-bone man was a great event as, for a jeely (jelly) jar, a large lollipop or a balloon could be obtained.

5 Hard Times

During the early 1930s, my father, an engineering fitter, suffered a total of six years' unemployment (four in succession). This was generally known as being 'on the buroo' (bureau). His weekly dole money, to keep the whole family, was 27s 3d (£1.36 in today's money) with 2s (10p) included for each of his two children. There were no additional payments such as housing benefit and it is a mercy that he neither smoked nor drank.

---

* This is how we pronounced the word.

Money was harboured in every possible way. Dad re-soled and re-heeled our shoes and cut our hair – the latter operation hated by Eric and me as he often tugged at the roots with the hand clippers. Meanwhile Mother darned, knit and mended. Similar to everyone else, our toilet paper was newsprint cut into squares, while string was always removed from brown paper parcels, and both the string and brown paper kept for future use. Toothpaste tubes, nearing their end, were slit open and the last drop used. And, when we took the tram home from town, we got off at the stop near the top of Rosefield Street as this was the 'fare stage' and a half-penny cheaper than the one nearer our house. Although some people, understandably, bought goods on hire purchase or 'tick', my parents were firmly against this and everything was paid for in cash.

Dad bought a newspaper from a shop in the Overgate, owned by a big bald man called Addison who spoke broad Dundee. As this was generally on a Saturday afternoon when we were on the way to a cinema, Mr Addison never failed to enquire if we were 'Awa tae the picturs?'

We were crossing the top of Glenagnes Road one Saturday afternoon, bound for the 'picturs', when Dad, who had been paid off that very morning, spotted Jeck Chalmers, his former sergeant in the City of Dundee Fortress Company of the Royal Engineers during the First World War, on the other side of Blackness Road. He crossed to speak to Jeck, and, on returning, we proceeded elated by the news that he been told he could start at Wallace Foundry on Monday. Unlike many tradesmen, Dad never went out with dirt-ingrained hands. On returning from work, he always scrubbed them thoroughly with grease solvent.

Unlike Dad, Grandad was a labourer who had done a variety of jobs, including that of crane driver. By the time I was about ten, he was a watchman at Blackness Foundry as he had only the state pension of, I believe, 10s (50p) a week. I would sometimes take his 'piece' (sandwiches) to him on a Sunday and go round the foundry with him, where the coal-fired furnaces were of particular interest.

When the Second World War began, he was 71 and worked the night shift in the munitions factory in Bellfield Street until he was dismissed on account of his age. This did not, however, end his working life as he then did a spell as night watchman at Robertson's furniture shop in Barrack Street. He liked nothing better than to visit the pub at the top of Rosefield Street. There, wearing the Black Watch badge of the old soldier, his penchant for spinning yarns must have made him popular as the landlord sent a wreath when he died.

With their lack of money, Christmas was difficult for my parents, and Dad later told me of a time when they had absolutely nothing for me until he won a toy monkey at the Green Market. Then, on returning home, he found that presents had come from Aunty

Ann and Mrs Mitchell and Lizzie and my grandparents. Believing in Santa Claus, I knew nothing of this and, on Christmas Eve, assiduously wrote a list of my requests to Santa on a white paper bag, with 'a bike' the main item. When the list was complete, the bag was blown up, stood on its open end in the fireplace, its top corners set alight and the pieces directed up the lum (chimney). Before going to bed and enduring a sleepless night because of my excitement, stockings and a pillowcase were laid out as receptacles for the presents. In the morning, an apple, an orange and a small golden string bag of chocolate coins wrapped in gold paper would be found among the gifts in the stockings, while new items of clothing, occupying much of the space in the pillow case, were disdainfully cast aside.

Inevitably, some of my playmates divulged that there was no Santa Claus and that it was only my parents who supplied the presents. I raced upstairs to seek confirmation of this from my father, but, when he did not give it and I eventually found it to be true, it undermined my trust in him. (As for the bike, I didn't get one until I was working. It was a second-hand one, and I twice fell badly from it when the front wheel caught in a tram line.)

Toys were stored in a fairly large and substantial wooden box, kept under our parents' bed. Known as 'The Big Box', it was generally on Sunday evenings that it was hauled out at our request. Eric and I would then empty it of its contents and have more fun sitting in it than playing with the toys!

Every second Sunday evening was, however, dreaded as Mother did the washing fortnightly, on a Monday, and, in anticipation of the chore, was always in a bad mood. As she also did the ironing on Monday, she was exhausted at the end of it and would look up, thankfully and proudly, at the laden pulley and sigh 'A' din' ('All done'). Meals were scrappy that day. When we were old enough, Eric and I turned the handle of the mangle at Logie Washhouse and helped with the dishes. Before we had electricity, the ironing was done with an iron heated on a gas ring.

Generally, we ate simply and well with stovies and rabbit included in our diet. Throughout the week, breakfast consisted of porridge, steeped during the night. On Sunday, bacon and egg was added, as we rose late and had no dinner (lunch). There was usually a stew for Sunday tea and at least one slice of bread had to be eaten before we could take one of the small cakes, in paper cups, which Mother baked herself. Clootie dumplings, with a thrup-ny (3d/1p) bit buried in them, was another of her specialities, but these appeared only on birthdays.

6 Victoria/Balgay Park

I must have been about nine when we got our first wireless. The arrival of this second-hand battery set caused great excitement. tuning in not only to the BBC but also stations such as Radio Athlone and Radio Luxembourg. When the wet battery/accumulator required charging, it was taken to Hill's (Hillie's) newspaper shop, a few yards up from the entrance to the close, where my grandfather purchased his bogey roll, cut off from a long strip by Mr Hill.

It was many years later that I gave my grandparents their first wireless. They didn't take to it at all, as Grandma couldn't understand the posh English accents of the speakers, which she disdainfully dismissed as 'ñough, ñough, ñough'.

Her own turn of speech sometimes puzzled me. She expressed surprise by saying 'Mercy me, surse (sirs)' and, when a number of children from other tenements had gathered in our back green, she would complain that 'Al and sundry comes t' play here.' It took me some time to work the meaning of that phrase, as I wondered who Al was!

Although my grandparents had a more complete command of Scots than either my parents or Eric and I did, we conversed in the dialect but switched to English when the need arose. This did not, however, mean that we spoke 'Dundee', which, with its 'eh' for 'yes' and its 'peh' for 'pie', was considered to be 'orrie'*, i.e. common in a derogatory sense. Orrie, pronounced 'ohrie', was also used for bad appearance and behaviour, and if we displayed these traits, Mother would say, 'Ye'd think ye cam' fae the Overgate.' Teachers were always addressed in English, but it was Scots in the playground.

We were fortunate to live near Victoria/Balgay Park, where we played football** in winter and cricket in summer. At the western end, there was a putting green and a pond, and the latter was a great attraction. It contained sticklebacks. Armed with small nets at the end of canes, we fished there and deposited our catch into jam jars. The jars were carried by string looped round their rims, and the prize catch was what we called a 'red gubber', as it had a red mark below its 'gub' (mouth). Engaged in this enthralling pursuit, I fell in one day. When I appeared dripping wet at the door of the washhouse – as it was my mother's washing day – I was promptly stripped and put into the tub.

Model yachts were sailed on the pond, and in summer there were rowing boats for hire. In winter, the pond

---

* The correct word is 'orra'. An orraman was an odd-job man on a farm, and the front page of the *Courier* carried numerous adverts for such men.
** At that time, football boots had uppers which reached well above the ankle, and I remember struggling up to the park with my brand-new first pair laced to the very top when the normal practice, which I soon adopted, was to lace them part way. To give a better grip of the ground, these boots had leather bars on the soles, although others had leather studs.

became a skating rink. My skates had wooden bases with steel blades inserted along their length. Only a leather strap secured the skate to the shoe at the front end but, in addition to a strap at the back, there was a screw that protruded from the wooden base and had to be wound into the heel of the shoe. This, of course, had a destructive effect on the shoe, so Mother was not amused.

The park was never so well used as at Easter, when the Protestants rolled their eggs on Saturday and the Catholics on Sunday. For those living in the eastern end of the town, the main venue was the Den o' Mains.

An ice-cream vendor, with his hand-pushed cart, often stood at the gate, and I remember a red-letter day when Walter Wilson stood us all tuppenny squashers – ice-cream and a snowball between the wafers. The gate and railings which adorned the park were removed during the Second World War, and, with food in short supply, part of the park was given over to plots on which schoolchildren, including Eric, cultivated vegetables.

Walter's (and Margaret's) younger brother, Jimmy Wilson, was Eric's pal, so we knew the family well. During the early part of the Second World War, when I was a piper in the Boys' Brigade, I saw an advert in the *Courier* stating that Piper Major William Ross, principal of the Army School of Piping at Edinburgh Castle, was to give free piping tuition to those selected at auditions held in Larg's Music Shop premises in Victoria Road. Believing this to be a good opportunity,

I went along with my chanter, but, as soon as the Pipe Major accepted me, the gentleman sitting beside him asked me for £1. To my reply 'I thought it was free?', he said that the pound was to help pay for Mr Ross' hotel accommodation in Dundee. This put a different aspect on the matter, and when Mother went with me to consult Mr Wilson, a piper in the Police Pipe Band, he pronounced in the negative, and that was that. Incidentally, when I gave my name to Pipe Major Ross, he responded with 'Sir Ian Malcolm of Poltalloch'. I had no idea what he meant, but soon learnt that I bore the same name as the clan chief.

An occasional ploy was to visit McDonald's Farm, which lay at some distance to the west of the park, where the workers were friendly and where we were allowed to skin a neep, divide it into pieces and dip them into a barrel of treacle before consumption! Incidentally, none of us had watches, so that we had to ask an adult for the time unless it was twelve noon, when the jute mill sirens – the bummers – used to sound all over Dundee.

7 Sunday Walks

Sunday was a day when people dressed in their best – the men in dark serge suits and the women in dark costumes or dresses – and Blackness Road was full of people carrying flowers and heading for Balgay Cemetery. My family didn't follow this practice, although Eric and I were made to dress in our kilts and go for a walk with our parents; we would much rather have stayed in the back green playing with our peers. If we went through Balgay Hill, we would stop for a drink at the ornate iron drinking fountain and sometimes try to throw a tennis ball over the bridge.

Another walk was round the docks, then open to the public. Ships which brought the jute from India would be tied up to the quay, and we would look up at lascars gazing down at us from their decks. One particular evening regarding the docks stands out in my memory. DP&L ships ploughed between Dundee and London, and I remember standing with my parents watching the *Perth* or *London* coming in to dock. As the ship's passengers were all on deck and there were numerous people on the quay, it seemed a great occasion to me. The ship had come from a far-off place called London! (Fares on these steamers, excluding food, were: first-class single cabin £2 2s 6d (£2.12½); second-class single cabin £1 7s 6d (£1.37½).

When it rained, the Albert Square museum and art galleries were favourite venues for Dundonians. On the ground floor of the museum were large stuffed animals, the skeleton of the whale washed ashore from the Tay, Egyptian mummies and human heads, shrunk by the Javaro Indians of the Amazon region, while among the exhibits upstairs were instruments of torture. In the art gallery the painting which impressed me most hung on the landing at the top of the stairs and showed Grace Darling and her father rowing out to assist the steamer *Forfarshire*, which had come to grief off the coast of Northumberland in 1838.

As Dundee was not the sprawling city that it is today, it was easy to walk into the countryside or take a tram to its terminus if going farther afield. And with few cars* on the roads, we could walk in safety – sometimes picking wild raspberries, strawberries, gooseberries and brambles, according to the season. Children are always interested in farm animals and the pigs kept in sties were a source of particular fascination. Armed with a set of wild flower cigarette cards, issued in packets of W.D. & H.O. Wills cigarettes, Dad would point out the various types of wild flowers which grew alongside the roads, while Mother, who had been brought up in country, described the crops in the fields. Invergowrie had a paper mill, and, if our walk took us in that direction, pieces of esparto grass could be seen beside the road, where they had fallen off lorries conveying the material from the docks.

---

* One of our ploys was to note their number plates.

In summer, many people took a bus to the foot of the Sidlaws, where they would spend the day picnicking. But, always energetic, Dad wanted to do more than that, and, in 1936, took Eric, my pal John Duncan and me over the Sidlaws to Glamis. It was a beautiful and enjoyable day spent in those wonderful hills, and we returned to Dundee by bus.

To most of us, Fife was only the part that we saw across the river. On a good Sunday, the Fifies/Tay ferries would be busy conveying Dundonians to Newport, either to sit on 'the braes' or walk farther afield – perhaps to Windmill Park or the Serpentine. The Fifies, which left from close to what is now Discovery Point, were the paddle steamers *Newport*, *Sir William High* and *B.L. Nairn*. The crossings were exhilarating and enjoyable, and it was fascinating to watch the movement of the ship's pistons through the skylight.

When I was very small, my mother took me for a sail to Newburgh, on the old *Cleopatra*, and, in later days, we would take the train to Wormit from the Esplanade station at the northern end of the Tay (railway) Bridge and walk the braes to Balmarino. And when I was in my early teens, my parents' friends, Peter and Mary Stark, and their daughter, Isobel, spent their weekends in a rented cottage in Balmarino which cost them something like 2s 6d (12½p). We were often asked over on a Sunday and still walked the braes from Wormit, although we had to use the central Tay Bridge station as the Esplanade station closed on 2 October 1939.

After the war, Peter and Mary became custodians of the Comerton Home, which is situated on the west side of the A92, south of Forgan, and funded by a Dundee charity to provide holidays for disadvantaged Dundee children.

I must have been three or four, when I went to Edinburgh with my grandmother and Mrs McKinnes. Nearing the Wormit end of the Tay (railway) Bridge, we had a clear view of the *Mars* lying at anchor on the seaward side. The *Mars*, an ex-Royal Navy ship and a training institution for boys since 1869, was broken up in 1929.

Mr and Mrs McKinnes lived next door to my grandparents with their three children – Jean, John and Philly (Philomena) – and our trip to Edinburgh was to visit her Italian parents, who owned a shop in the vicinity of the High Street in the Old Town. What I remember of the visit is sitting at a table, on which was a massive plate of spaghetti, with a number of people. The shop sold 'lucky potatoes' – sweetmeats, shaped like potatoes, covered with cocoa and so-called because you might find a half-penny inside. I was given a 'potato', but, like most of them, it was not lucky.

Mr (David) McKinnes, the son of the old lady who lived on the ground floor, had served in France during the First World War and, when he was in his cups on a Saturday night, he would go on about crossing the Somme carrying a full pack. He was always pleasant, and if I met him in his inebriated state he would try to say something funny, although the most he could generally muster was 'Mickey Mouse'!

John McKinnes, a slightly built lad of about Eric's age, took up boxing when in his teens. One evening he sat beside Eric in Forest Park Cinema when the boy behind Eric put his feet on Eric's seat. When Eric pushed them off, the boy became threatening and put them back on. Eventually, John, as small as he was, turned round, grabbed the boy and asked him to step outside. This settled the matter. The boy threw in the towel!

8 A Holiday

For most of my grandfather's working life, his summer holiday was one week without pay, and this was amicably accepted by the workers as they thought it reasonable that an employer should not pay them when they did not work. Christmas Day was a normal working day, and this obtained throughout the first ten years or so of my own working life.

By the 1930s, the summer holiday week was 'with pay', but, with slender resources, most people spent it going for, what was called, 'a day here and there'. Broughty Ferry, reached by tram, was a favourite venue, and the beach, devoid of the heaped-up sand and rough grass which grows on it today, would be crowded. Those who could afford to go away didn't go far, and a next-door neighbour went annually to Kirriemuir.

We, however, didn't go as far as that in 1933. Aunty Meg was kind enough to let us have her house in Invergowrie for a week, when she and her daughter were away, and Eric and I had as good a time as any of today's children being taken to such far away places as Spain or Florida.

The house, which stands in a row of houses on the north side of the main road, had a large vegetable garden stretching down to the Gowrie Burn. Eric and I spent endless hours in the burn, damming it and hunting for small fish. A larger house stood next door to the west, and, tempted by the large apples which hung on the tree whose branches overhung our fence, I was helping myself one day when a lady caught me. She was, however, a pleasant lady and spoke without rancour, which nevertheless caused me considerable embarrassment. But that was not the end of it as, when I was in the garden the following day, she further embarrassed me by calling to me and handing a basket full of apples over the fence. That lady, a retired teacher called Miss Gardiner, knew her psychology!

We did not exactly have the house to ourselves as Aunty Meg had a boarder – a young man who worked as a porter at the railway station. Eric and I slept in the front upstairs room, as did the young man, and I would lie awake amused by the lights of passing traffic as they moved across the ceiling in the direction opposite to the one in which the vehicles travelled. We accompanied our boarder when he went swimming one evening in the harbour at Kingoodie. Other young people, dressed as I was in their full-length swimming costumes, were also in. But, in spite of my father's exhortations from his more comfortable position on the sea wall, I couldn't swim and was glad to get out of the freezing water. On another occasion, he, Eric and I waded out in the mud when the tide was out and were surprised at the distance we got from the shore. The mud was over our ankles, and my grandfather used to tell of a gentleman who waded regularly in the mud at Dundee as it is apparently good for the feet.

This, however, was not my first holiday with my parents. We had been to Methil in 1928, when we had lodged in a miner's house. And all I remember is standing on the bed trying to get a sound out of our host's bagpipes and holding up my celluloid windmill into the breeze when on the open top of a tram which ran to Kirkcaldy. Also, we had been to Stanley, in 1930, when Eric was only eighteen months. And all I remember of that holiday is picking rasps by the side of the road and feeding them to Eric in his pram, on which a board provided a seat for me, aged five and a half.

I would go to Ninewells with other children. This was more or less the western extremity of Dundee, where stone steps descended to the shore and to a path which lead to the Levelies where the beach was not so stony. Mother sometimes took Eric and me to picnic at the Levelies, but our favourite place was the Den o' Fowlis/Spinkie Den. The latter was not overgrown as it is today, and we went some way into it to our preferred open area where we could play in the burn or swing on the trees. We also made annual excursions to the Den to gather wild raspberries, which grew in abundance and were consigned to Mother's copper-lined jeely (jelly) pan the same evening.

To get to the Den o' Fowlis, we walked to the junction of Liff Road and Coupar Angus Road, in Lochee, where McGibbon's bus, running to Liff, had its terminus conveniently close to Jean Phin's candy shop. I later took this bus to visit David Mitchell, a schoolmate when at Logie Central School. David's father was a gardener at West Green Asylum (now Liff Hospital), and their cottage stood at the western end of the grounds, some way down from the crossroads where I descended from the bus.

I always gladly accepted the invitations to visit David's home as we had the freedom of the grounds and his mother not only fed us well but also allowed us, together with his sister, Jean, to jump about on the settee in the living room! The highlight of the year at West Green, however, was the Sports Day, which was always well attended and great fun. I particularly remember the greasy pole and a race where people were wheeled in handcarts and buckets of water emptied on to them if they failed to negotiate a hazard. Attending the Sports Day was also a lesson to me. At other times, the

Asylum was so mysteriously silent from the outside that I thought that the inmates would all be seriously mentally disturbed if not dangerous. Seeing many of them enjoying and participating in the sports altered my opinion.

9 Cinemas

In these pre-television days, the cinema was king and, similar to all cities, Dundee abounded in them. My father took me on my first visit to one when I was about four. This was to the Kinnaird in Bank Street, and he always afterwards made fun of the fact that I had no interest in the film, but continually asked to be taken to see the 'bonnie lavies' again! We generally went to the cinema on Saturday afternoons – to the Kinnaird, La Scala in the Murraygate, the Majestic in the Seagate and to the Kings in the Cowgate, where the organist, together with his Wurlitzer organ, ascended from somewhere down below and was greeted with applause. As the performances were continuous, people came in at any time and, when, during the next showing, they recognized a scene, they said, 'This is where we came in' and left. As soon as a performance ended, there was a general scurrying for the exits before the National Anthem was played, but those who didn't succeed in reaching them, then stood still until it finished.

Green's Playhouse, in the Nethergate, opened in 1936 with Anna Neagle starring in *Sixty Glorious Years*. With its 4,100 seats, it was the largest cinema in Britain. I remember pamphlets being distributed from an open-backed lorry outside Logie School advertising an Al Jolson film. I also recall standing in a long queue at the Palace Theatre, near the back of the Queen's Hotel, with my mother to see one of the early Shirley Temple films.

Our local cinemas were Forest Park in Forest Park Road, the Princess in the Hawkhill, the Queen's in Well Road, Gray's in Shepherd's Loan and the Alhambra in Bellfield Street, where the cheapest seats cost tuppence (2d/1p). In Gray's, these seats consisted of two red cushioned forms so close to the screen that you had to look almost directly upwards. My grandparents paid my entrance to the Alhambra on Friday evenings, when the audience consisted almost entirely of boys. Before the performance, the place was bedlam during the showing of adverts, but we all knew that the last one was for Lavapine and, as this signalled that the show was about to start, a great cheer went up when it appeared. If boys were making a nuisance of themselves during the performance, a checker/attendant would shine his torch on them and threaten eviction. There was always a short film prior to the main one, and this often took the form of a serial such as *Rin Tin Tin*. That wonderful Alsatian dog always saved the day, and each episode ended with a cliff-hanging scene with the hero, Frankie Darro, in dire straits. There was a period, however, when the Alhambra attracted a more respectable audience, as live performances of Shakespeare's plays took place there. Later renamed the State and still existing as the Whitehall Theatre, the door which we, the kids, used to enter is now blocked up.

A cinema which we would go to only if something special were being shown was the Britannia in Small's Wynd. The 'Brit' was even rougher than the 'Ally' on a Friday night, and orange peel would fly about while the juvenile audience waited impatiently for the show to start. If you were foolish enough to complain, you were liable to find yourself on the receiving end of a hammering.

Among our favourite stars were the cowboys – Tim McCoy, Randolph Scott and Hopalong Cassidy – and the comedians – Laurel and Hardy, Andy Clyde, Wallace Beery, Leon Errol, the Bowery Boys and the Marx Brothers. Although popular, Bette Davis, Katherine Hepburn, Fred Astaire and Ginger Rogers and William Powell and Myrna Loy were more to the taste of adults.

10 Shops

Our everyday needs were supplied by the local shops, and my mother put in an order every week at the branch of the Dundee Eastern Cooperative Society (The Sosh) at the foot of Peddie Street. This was done by her writing out the order in a book, which was supplied, and I would take it to the shop and place it in the receptacle on the counter. The order was then delivered to the house free of charge and, most importantly, the dividend mounted up.

Among the local shops were Taylor's, the fruiterer and confectioner who sold tiger nuts, and Robertson's, the chemist, where we could buy locust beans and liquorice sticks. We applied the name 'liquorice' to the dried root of the shrub, chewed and then discarded, and also to the jet-black confectionery. A jingle concerning the latter, which we called 'sugarelly' and was sometimes shaken in a glass container containing water, went 'Sugarelly water, black as the lum, gie me a peen (pin) and you'll get some.'

Regarding medicines, Eric and I were given a daily tablespoon of cod liver oil and malt in winter. When it was considered that our systems required a 'clearing out', we got a dose of the nauseating sulphur and treacle – the former often resulting in an equally obnoxious odour! Brown iodine was applied to cuts and skinned knees, and, the more it hurt, the more effective it was deemed to be. For bruises and sprains,

Sloan's Liniment, with the drawing of a bearded man on its box, was always to hand, and a whisky toddy given for head colds. If, however, the cold was in the chest, and which Grandad called a hoast, a mustard poultice would be applied.

A piece of butter,* dipped in sugar, was given for a tickle in the throat, but the main remedy for a sore throat was gargling with a salt-water solution. If, however, Grandad peered into our mouths and pronounced 'Your hass is doon,' he would place salt on the back of a wet teaspoon and apply it to the distended, inflamed hass (uvula). During our early years at school, we were occasionally infected by head lice. Mother disposed of them by combing our hair with a small, almost square and close-toothed bone comb, and lice caught in the comb were revealed when it was tapped on a plate.

Clothes were bought in town, where there were so many excellent shops. Draffen's was undoubtedly the premier shop, but others such as D.M. Brown's, GL's (G.L. Wilson's), Smith Brothers, Caird's, Menzies and the main shop of the DECS in the Seagate were not far behind. A feature of the DECS shop which interested me was that cash and receipts flew, in tubes, between the counters and an office upstairs. In the Overgate, Birrell's was a favourite place for shoes, while Greenhill, the best-known chemist in Dundee, sold all sorts of drinks, including his famous sarsaparilla. According

---

* Butter was also used to remove tar from our hands.

to a joke, a man entered Greenhill's shop asking for a laxative. 'Where do you live and are you going straight home?' enquired the chemist. 'The tap o' the Hull (Hilltown),' replied the man and said he was going straight home. 'Right,' said Greenhill and, after mixing a potion, the man drank it on the spot. When he entered the shop some days later, the chemist asked him how he had got on. 'No bad,' he replied, 'but ye didna gie me time tae louse my galluses (release my braces).'

In summer, Eric and I wore Clark's crepe-soled, leather sandals, and a new jacket was never worn before Mother 'handselled' it by placing a thrup-ny bit or sixpenny piece in a pocket to bring good luck.

Similar to many older Dundonians, I have always regretted the total destruction of the old Overgate. The houses were undoubtedly slums, but there were many good shops and the street could have been renovated and preserved, as was the High Street in Edinburgh. The Overgate was particularly lively on a Saturday night with people shopping or eating peas and chips at the canvas 'buster' stalls. We were often in town then, and Eric and I liked going to the wooden-floored Woolworth's in the Murraygate to search for American comics, sold in numbered sets. Although Woolworth's advertised that they sold 'nothing over 6d (2½p)', this did not mean that all items could be bought at this price. For example, people who could not afford to go to an optician bought spectacles by the trial-and-error system of selecting a pair they could see best with and then paying, perhaps, 6d for each leg and the same for the frame and each lens. Grandma bought me a single, no ball-bearings roller skate in this way as she considered it too dangerous for me to have the pair! The layout of Woolworth's stores was quite different from their layout today. The goods were displayed on horizontal counters and, as check-out points lay in the future, there was an assistant behind each counter to take your money.

On the way home, we would walk up the busy Hawkhill (known as the Hackie) with its many shops below the tenement houses. Similar to the Overgate, this area was demolished and a community destroyed – this time by the advent of Dundee University.

Regarding spectacles, I have worn them since the age of four. My father noticed that, when I was tired, there was a trace of a squint in one eye, and this resulted in Mother taking me to a clinic in the Nethergate. As I visited this clinic on other occasions, I remember Dr McGillivray, the eye specialist, very well. A tall, bespectacled, balding and severe-looking man, sitting on a high stool, he never addressed a pleasantry to me. He prescribed spectacles to cure the squint, which they did, but his forecast that I would be able to dispense with them when I was fourteen proved incorrect. My first and all subsequent pairs of spectacles were provided by small and cheerful W.S. Marshal Strachan, who had his shop at 161 Hilltown. Known to us as

Wullie, he had worked beside my father in Blackness Foundry before qualifying as an optician.

I was seven when I took ill. Dr Morgan diagnosed scarlet fever and a nurse carried me downstairs in a blanket to the waiting ambulance, which took me to Kings Cross Hospital. On arrival, I was deposited in a bed next to Alistair Dodds, the boy I sat beside at school.

As I was not that bad, I don't think I was in the hospital for more than three weeks. The young nurses were very kind. We had plenty to occupy ourselves with and, on visiting days, my parents smuggled cream cookies to me through the lavatory window. As far as hospital food was concerned, I liked it so much that, when my mother announced that she had been told that she could collect me on Monday, I said not to come before dinnertime as we got hash that day! I was only days back home, however, when Eric was carted off to Kings Cross with the same complaint – but, for a three-year-old, hospitalisation is a traumatic experience.

11 The Baths

As we had no bathroom in the house, Eric and I went to Corporation baths at the top of Guthrie Street and, later, to the baths and swimming pools at the Shore. To get to the latter, we walked through the Royal Arch, which was later demolished to provide access roads for the Tay Road Bridge. The baths were divided into three classes: the 1st had everything you would expect; the 2nd was less palatial, and the water controls in the passageway were operated by an attendant; while the 3rd class was downright spartan, with a communal mirror in the passageway.

We went to the 2nd class, where the great sport was bawling out for more cold water for, say, No.7, occupied by a friend, when you were in another bath. The attendant would oblige, and a howl would go up from No.7 when cold water poured into his tub. It was not unknown, however, for the attendant to retaliate by admitting cold water into the bath of the joker.

Many of us made use of the free swimming pool at the Coup, located near the railway footbridge and close to Magdalen Green railway station. This pool was beautifully built of red sandstone, and there were cubicles in which to undress. As the water was merely taken from the Tay, it was perishing cold. When Alice, Nan Mollison (who lived on the first landing of our tenement) and I went there one Sunday morning, we had the pool to ourselves, yet, on a summer's day, it would be full of boys creating bedlam. (Nan, who always looked the picture of health, died of tuberculosis at about the age of seventeen. Alice contracted the same disease when she was twenty-two, in her knee. As replacements were then unheard of, the affected part was removed, and she was left with a stiff leg and a slight limp.)

In the early years, we went to the 2nd class pool at Dundee corporation baths, but to the 1st class when we became more solvent. The 2nd class had neither springboard nor diving platform, and there was a separate pool for ladies. If they were busy, a time limit was imposed in all pools. This put a strain on the attendants in the men's pools and, in the first class, when they blew their whistles to indicate time was up, many of the boys secreted themselves in the 'hotties' – a spacious room with low porcelain tubs and showers. Eventually, not able to locate the boys concerned, an attendant would appear in the 'hotties' with clothes from a cubicle in his arms, threatening that they would be thrown into the pool if the culprit didn't own up!

The salt water in the pools was filtered, sterilized and heated to 72 °F, but, for me, the main attraction of the 1st class was that, along one side, it had rings suspended from the ceiling by ropes, so that, like Tarzan, you could swing over its whole length. To attend the baths, Mother would give us the money plus a half-penny for the return tram half-fares. But, as a chip shop at the foot of Peddie Street sold half-penny bags, we sometimes walked home and bought chips. This shop also sold (potato) fritters – something never seen these days.

Before Eric was born, my mother took me regularly to see her parents, the McQuatties, who had moved from Drumgeith to Mains of Gray Farm – south of Liff and seen in the background of J. McIntosh Patrick's painting 'The Brook, Benvie'.* We went by bus to Invergowrie and walked by way of the Deil's Stane, reputed to have been thrown from Fife by the Deil (Devil). My maternal grandparents' house was in a row of farmer workers' cottages, behind which was a level area before the pastureland, full of buttercups and marguerites, descended to the Benvie Burn. On a good summer's day, the tea would be eaten from a table set out at the back of the house, and I loved running about in the pasture. It seemed that I also took delight in investigating the midden, a stonewalled enclosure into which household rubbish was deposited, and they all thought it hilarious when they found me in there. My only recollection of my maternal grandmother is of a stout, white-haired lady lying in bed, and it was several years later before I learned that this was because she was terminally ill.

12 Comics

The first comic which I got was *Chicks' Own* – a comic for toddlers. Mother must always have taken me to visit her parents on the same day of the week, as when we returned to the house I immediately went to the tea cosy, at the foot of their bed, where my father hid it.

---

* I always wonder why it was not called 'The Burn'.

Other comics which Eric and I later got, and read also by Dad, were *Comic Cuts, Chips, Larks* and *Film Fun* – the last, with Laurel and Hardy on the front page, was smaller but thicker, and cost a penny more. Later still, it was the *Adventure, Hotspur, Rover* and *Wizard.* The *Adventure* was my favourite, and, shortly after beginning to get it, I entered a competition for a stamp album. I could hardly contain myself waiting for the results. Seeing this, my mother tried to shield me from disappointment by saying that there would be thousands of entrants. But, lo and behold, my name was in the list of winners!

With the approach of the Second World War, more work was available, and consequently money more plentiful, so that we spent a week in Comrie in 1937. We stayed in the bungalow of Mr and Mrs McGrory and their small daughter, Elizabeth. Mother bought our food and Mrs McGrory prepared the meals. Armed with canes and bent pins, Eric and I fished unsuccessfully in the River Earn, but one day a man, who had a good catch, gave us a fine trout. On the way back to our digs, another unsuccessful angler, with good tackle, admired the fish and questioned us as to where we had caught it. We let him believe that we had indeed caught it, but, unbeknown to us, this man knew our father, and when they met a day or so later, the true facts were revealed to him.

The Earn was a magnet to us, and it was in it that I learned to swim. It was a beautiful day and Dad, never willing to sit about, wanted us to go to Glen Lednock. We rebelled and elected for the Earn, so that Dad went on his own. I learned to swim by pushing off from an embedded stone into about eighteen inches of water, and suddenly I knew I had the technique! It was a momentous occasion for me – and many years before I became aware that I had learned by what is known as the Shallow Water Method. At the end of our week, I was very loath to leave Comrie.

The *Dandy* appeared in 1937 and the *Beano* in 1938. Regretfully, I didn't buy the first issue of either, as they are worth a great deal today. I remember the latter appeared during the holiday we had in Belfast. This was the year of the Empire Exhibition in Glasgow's Bellahouston Park, and we went to it before boarding the *Royal Ulsterman* at the Broomielaw. My only recollections of the Exhibition are a miniature version of the Victoria Falls, and Mother accompanying Eric and me on the helter-skelter/roller coaster.

The crossing to Belfast, on the other hand, is well remembered. We almost missed the ship by waiting at the wrong quay, and the already half-raised gangway had to be re-lowered to allow us to board. However, the fact that we were the last to board proved most propitious for us as our tickets were not checked. No doubt because we were well dressed – with Eric and me in our kilts – we were directed into a large communal room on an upper deck although we had only steerage tickets. My father had absolutely no knowledge of how steerage passengers travelled. They were accommodated in the hold, on which we looked down from our deck. It would have been bad enough just being down that hold, but drunks made the situation worse, and when fighting broke out during the night, sailors had to be sent down to restore order.

13 Friends and Relations

Dundee had an excellent transport system, provided mainly by Corporation double-decker trams, devoid of advertisements, and sporting a pleasant green and white livery with the city coat of arms emblazoned on their sides. With electric motors at both ends, they did not have to be turned round. At the termini, the seat backs were pushed into the reverse position, the roof connection to the overhead electric cable changed over to the cable of the return route, and the driver walked through the tram to the other motor. As the driver's platform was spacious, prams and other large items were accommodated there, free of charge. The High Street stop for the Blackness tram lay between the north-east corner of the City Square and Castle Street, and I never pass the place without thinking how busy it used to be around half past five on a weekday, when people boarded the trams carrying the 'Tully' – the *Evening Telegraph*.

A tram, heading for Downfield, came down Blackness Road roughly every four minutes, and when visiting our friends, Mrs Mitchell and her daughter, Lizzie, who lived at 1 Harriet Street, we took the tram to Dura Street and walked the rest of the way. This tenement, where a car park now stands, was similar to ours in most respects, but above the Mitchell's house – an end one on the top storey – was a garret in which lived an old maiden lady called Miss Clark. (No doubt this was common in Dundee as there was a popular song, the verses of which ended with 'Oh, deary me, what shall I dae if I dee an auld maid in a garret'.) The Mitchells and Miss Clark used the same door on the plat, with the formers' front door immediately on the left as you entered; directly ahead were wooden stairs leading to the garret. Another way in which that tenement differed from our own was that clothes were dried on lines slung over pulleys attached to windows and which ran to a large wooden pole in the back green. Lizzie was a forewoman in Keillor's Factory, famous throughout the world for its marmalade. She often referred to the brand 'Little Chip'. As sweets were also made, we seldom left the house without a bag of rejects known in the business as 'throw-outs'.

Although I was not aware of it, it was not an uncommon sight to see children waiting outside a public house while their parents were imbibing. The back window of Mrs Mitchell's overlooked the pub at the corner of Dura Street and Balmore Street, and she pointed this out to me while saying, 'You'll never hae tae dae that.' Incidentally, when visiting anyone, a small gift, usually a quarter-pound packet of tea, was taken. And, although this was the normal practice, the recipient always expressed mild surprise while saying something like, 'You shouldn't have bothered.'

During the 1920s and '30s many young men tried to escape the Depression by emigrating to the United States, and Mrs Mitchell's son, Hector, an engineering fitter, was one of them. This was in 1929, and my mother and I were among those on the station platform seeing him off. Throughout the many years that we visited them, Mother would ask Mrs Mitchell if she had heard from Hector. But he neglected his mother shamefully, and the answer was almost always in the negative. Nevertheless, after over forty years of holding only menial jobs in Pittsburgh, Hector came home to retire.

Other friends were a well-known Lochee family, the Beggs, who lived in the tenement (no plats and since demolished) at 24 South Road, where from a back window they could see the predominantly Irish settlement known as Tipperary. As it would have been necessary to take a tram into the city centre then another to Lochee, we walked to their house, which was larger than ours but necessary for the large family. Mr (Joe) Begg, a widower by the time I knew him, had three daughters and four sons. Joanne, the eldest, had left home by then and Bob left shortly to work in Bristol, so that my recollection is of Meg, Betty, Chick, young Joe and Jimmy, who was about my age. Mr Begg, an elder of St Luke's Kirk, regaled us with stories of what he had said to the minister at Presbytery meetings. A meal was always provided. Although it was still reasonably early in the evening, Jimmy would get into his pyjamas in another room and go to bed behind a curtain in the room in which we all sat talking, because he delivered papers before going to school in the morning. Today, it seems that notice has generally to be given of a visit, but, in these days, without telephones, visits were almost always spontaneous, yet there was never any thought of visitors leaving without having a meal. (My first visit to the Beggs was when they lived in a row of cottages, with what had once been a communal well behind them, in Heron's Lane. And as my grandmother's parents had lived there, I presume this is how my parents came to know them.)

Relations whom we visited on rare occasions were the McFaulds, who also lived in a row of cottages in Lochee. Mr John McFauld, a cousin of my father, had lost a leg in the First World War and his son, John but known as Jackie, was to lose his life, on HMS *Dunedin*, in the Second World War. Robbie, their other son was about the same age as I was and also attended Logie Central School. Mr McFauld's father, also John but known as Jeck, was married to my grandfather's sister, Agnes. They lived quite near us in a detached house in Milnbank Road, and it may have been another of their sons who died in a drowning accident in the United States and bequeathed to them the sum of, I believe, £1,000. This was an enormous sum in those days, but Jeck had little trouble in going through it. One red-letter day, which my grandfather talked about ever afterwards with great enjoyment, was when Jeck hired a taxi for the day and took Agnes and my grandparents for a drive in the country. Arriving at the Beech Hedges, at Meikleour, Jeck had the driver stop. He and Grandad, no doubt with a good drink inside them, tried to throw stones over the Hedges (a long line of beech trees). Seeing what they were up to, other drivers stopped, and soon there was a line of cars with their occupants joining in the sport.

When Jeck and Agnes died, my grandparents inherited a gramophone in a beautiful mahogany case with a compartment to hold the 78 rpm records. These were mostly of Scottish music, but an unusually large one was of music hall songs, among which was Charlie Coburn singing 'The Man Who Broke The Bank At Monte Carlo'. There were no volume controls on gramophones in those days. The sound could be reduced only by stuffing a cloth into the speaker, so this may be the origin of the expression 'Put a sock in it (Shut up).'

Aunty Agnes and Uncle Jim Chalmers lived in the row of cottages at the bottom, eastern side, of Peddie Street. Sometime in the 1930s, their elder daughter, Bessie, married a farmer called Smith. The ceremony

TOP. Grandma and Grandad at home, c. 1920.

ABOVE. Mother with me, Craig Pier, 1925.

TOP. Mother, Dad and me, c. 1927.

ABOVE. *L to R*. Stuart Elder, unidentified, David Durie,
? McGregor, me, Alice Durie and Alec Elder, 'Doon the Backies', c. 1929.

TOP. On Victoria Park pond, c. 1929.

ABOVE. Grandma and Grandad, Balgay Hill, 1930.

TOP. 219 Blackness Road, with hoardings, in 1972. Looked much the
same as pre-war, apart from the TV aerials, cars and without tram lines.

ABOVE. 219 Blackness Road (faraway tenement on the left). Logie School, centre.

TOP. Rear view of 219 Blackness Road (far left). Our house is first
right at the top of the circular staircase. Washhouse (with chimney) and
wartime Anderson Shelter in back green, 1961.

ABOVE. View from our plat. Logie Church Hall is left of centre
with Logie Church adjacent left, 1961.

TOP. Grandad on our plat, c. 1950.

ABOVE. Eric and me, Victoria Park, 1930.

TOP. Blackness Public School, 1972.

ABOVE. At Balgay Hill drinking fountain, c. 1935.

Two classes, Blackness Public School, c. 1932. L to R. *Front row*: James Miller, Bobby Brodie, James Scott, Betty Young, unidentified, Helen Sheridan, unidentified, ? McCauley, Charlie Small, Ronald Brown, James Christie, James Binnie. *Second row*: Kenny Robertson, Alice Durie, unidentified, Dorothy Kinnes, Betty Sherriff, unidentified, Barbara ?, unidentified, Margaret Petrie, me. *Third row*: unidentified, unidentified, Myna Cross, unidentified, Isa Driscoll, unidentified, ? Swan, unidentified in uniform of Industrial School, unidentified, unidentified, Georgina Ramsay, Helen Dingwall, Norman MacLeod. *Back row*: Sandy Dunsmore, David Marr, Kenny Paterson, Alistair Dodds, Billy Burry, David Carey, Robbie Davidson, Ronald Boyd, Billy Brown, John Duncan, Jimmy Smith.

TOP. Eric and me, Sunday walk, c. 1935.

ABOVE. Me, John Duncan and Eric in the Sidlaws, 1936.

TOP. Dalmally Station, evening excursion to Oban, 1937.

ABOVE. Where we fished on the Coup.

TOP. Royal Arch design on ashtray

ABOVE. 'Fifey' *B.L. Nairn*, 1945.

TOP. Joe Begg (Jr), me, Meg Begg, Jimmy Begg, Mother,
Eric and Joe Begg, Edinburgh Zoo, 1935.

ABOVE. *L. to R*: Jack Doig, son of teacher, unidentified, unidentified, me, Jimmy Begg,
John Duncan, William Husband and Archie Duncan, Cheddar Gorge, 1938.

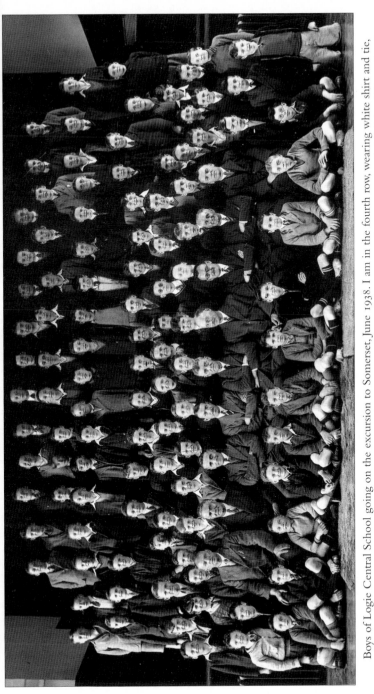

Boys of Logie Central School going on the excursion to Somerset, June 1938. I am in the fourth row, wearing white shirt and tie, with John Duncan on my left. Robbie McFauld is fourth from the right in the front row and Jimmy Begg is behind the fifth teacher from the left. Teachers, *L to R*: Messrs Simpson, Burnett, Smith, Mollison, Doig, Kitto, Thomson, Adamson and Legge.

RIGHT AND MIDDLE RIGHT.
Former Pupils' Association
membership card
1939/40.

BELOW RIGHT.
Excursion ticket

BELOW.
BB Swimming Certificate, 1941.

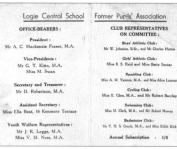

Logie Central School | Former Pupils' Association

OFFICE-BEARERS :

President :
Mr A. C. Mackenzie Fraser, M.A.

Vice-Presidents :
Mr G. T. Kitto, M.A.
Miss M. Swan

Secretary and Treasurer :
Mr D. Robertson, M.A.

Assistant Secretary :
Miss Ella Beat, 16 Kenmore Terrace

Youth Welfare Representatives :
Mr J. R. Legge, M.A.
Miss V. M. Ness, M.A.

**CLUB REPRESENTATIVES
ON COMMITTEE :**

Boys' Athletic Club :
Mr W. Johnston, B.Sc., and Mr Charles Hutton

Girls' Athletic Club :
Miss S. S. Reid and Miss Betty Soutar

Rambling Club :
Miss A. M. Yeaman, M.A., and Miss Alice Lawson

Cycling Club :
Miss E. Glen, M.A., and Mr Robert Barclay

Swimming Club :
Miss M. Clark, M.A., and Mr Robert Murray

Badminton Club :
Mr T. D. S. Gracie, M.A., and Miss Edith Kirk

Annual Subscription - 1/6

Eric, me and Mother, Balgay Hill, 1941.

TOP. View of the Nethergate from the top of the Old Steeple (St Mary's Tower), 1951.

ABOVE. The former A. and S. Henry building in Victoria Road. Arched entrances led to the loading bays and the rectangular entrance, to marble staircase and office. The works entrance was by the lane between the near end of the building and the now disused church.

TOP. The former entrance to the Palais (de Danse)

ABOVE. Photo for Special PMG Certificate in Radiotelegraphy, June 1943.

was conducted in the manse and the reception held in the house. Mother, Eric and I attended the reception in the crowded house, where a gramophone, playing 78 rpm records and with a large horned speaker, provided the music. As was the normal practice, coins were thrown from the taxi in which the bridal couple left. Mother had given Eric and me strict instructions not the join in the scramble, so we stood reluctantly by until she eventually relented. If a couple left without throwing 'maiks' (half-pennies and pennies), the kids shouted 'Roosty (rusty) pockets' after them!

When I was about three, my grandmother and I paid a visit to my grandfather's widowed sister, Annie Faren, who lived in Isles Lane, off the Hawkhill. Although I was given the luxury of drinking tea out of a saucer (never allowed at home), my continued movements so irritated Annie that she raged, 'Can ye no' sit still, bairn.' In retrospect, perhaps this was because she had a horsehair settee – the protruding hairs of which could jag bare legs.

14 Logie Central School

Logie Church, where the minister was the Rev. Dr Bartlett, stood in Scott Street, facing the northern end of Glenagnes Road. From an early age, I attended the Sunday school where Miss Edwards was superintendent, then the Life Boys and, finally, the Boys' Brigade (BB) Eleventh Company. Miss Blyth was captain of the Life Boys – an organisation for boys too young to join the BB. The uniform was a round, navy blue sailor's hat, bound by a ribbon bearing the name Life Boys, and a navy blue jersey with their badge sewn on. The Eleventh Company had a bugle band, but, as I was never able to get a bugle and some of the boys were too rough for my liking, I decided to leave. Mr Steele was the captain and, when I informed him of my decision, he tried to entice me to stay by offering a bugle. I had already learned that I could get the pipes by joining the Third YMCA Company, in Constitution Road, and I remained in that company for many years. The Eleventh wore the normal pillbox hat, while the Third wore a forage cap and the St Andrews Company, the glengarry.

Logie Church Hall, which still stands, was adjacent to the church and opposite to what was known as Hennie Parkie. This was where the BB met and where Sunday school Christmas parties, concerts and slide shows were held. I attended a slide show denouncing the Japanese invasion of Manchuria as well as a concert where, dressed in Victorian style, a young couple sang 'She's My Lady Love'. The latter has particularly remained in my memory because the young man, Roy Wilson, was destined to die a few years later when flying with the RAF.

My father was a member of the Loyal Order of Ancient Shepherds, and I attended the Christmas parties held in their premises in the Seagate. The Noble Duke of York was lead by a stout Mrs Forbes whose 'tie yi yi yi yahs' were never to be forgotten. The party ended with a silent film show given by Mr Norman Brown, a professional photographer with premises at 19/20 Barrack Street. Mr Brown chose his films well, as Charlie Chaplin featured largely in the show.

Doctors' bills had to be paid, but I believe that medical insurance was one of the benefits of Shepherds' membership. Dental treatment came free at the dental hospital in Park Place, where the drills were foot-driven by the students. Sugary sweets cause tooth decay. We weren't overindulged, but sweets we did eat included MacCowan's Highland toffee. These bars, the wrapper of which sported a Highland cow, could not be recommended to anyone with false teeth! It was only a year or two before his death that my grandfather visited a dentist for the first time, and, as this was in the post-war period, dentistry was free. Prior to this, a painful tooth was extracted with pliers, and his nicotine-stained teeth lasted to the end of his days.

Moving up from Blackness School to Logie Central was a major step. All jotters and books had to be bought – the former from Chambers' paper shop at the western junction of Blackness Road and Rosefield Street and the latter, second-hand, from Frank Russell's Bookshop in Barrack Street. Prior to going to Logie, I wondered how there could be such a subject as bookkeeping. What was there to learn specially about keeping books?

At neither Blackness nor Logie did I wear school uniform. At Blackness, it was a home-knitted jersey and tie to match. At Logie, it was, generally, a navy blue suit, white shirt (tucked in!) and tie. And I did not possess a pair of long trousers until I was sixteen – two years after I left school. I don't recall any of the boys at Logie wearing a school blazer, but almost all the girls wore gymslips in the school colours.

Our initiation to Logie was being thrown into the bushes behind the school by our seniors. In these days, there were two intakes a year – a sensible system which was dispensed with many years later on the spurious grounds of reducing administration work. The top commercial class (French section) was 1FM2, and I was put into 1FM1 (First year, February intake, Mixed, science section).

Among the teachers I had, and whose names I remember, were Mr Robertson (English), Miss Ness (English), Mr Frank Smith (arithmetic), Mr Doig (algebra), Mr Adamson (commercial), Mr Burnett (gym), Miss Guild (science), Mr Kitto (science), Miss Martin (history), Mr Cluckie (geography) and Miss Yeaman (Bible).

Miss Ness, who was very strict, didn't suffer fools gladly, and in spite of having over 80 per cent in an exam, she belted me for what she believed to be a stupid mistake. We had to put into prose a verse about Dick the shepherd blowing his nail and milk being frozen in the pail, and I had written 'Dick (the owl)'. 'You know perfectly well that Dick isn't the owl,' she fumed. What she didn't know, and gave me no opportunity to explain, was that I thought brackets could be used to delete words and was neater than stroking them out with the pen.

Although cheerful, Mr Smith was liable to be sarcastic. I always felt wary of him, and one day he lost his temper at Isa Driscoll and chased her round the classroom!

To begin with, I had a young male teacher for algebra. I liked the teacher, but my exam marks were very poor. Then this teacher fell ill and his place was taken by Mr Doig, a tall, elderly, bespectacled martinet whose eyes roamed the class seeking out those not paying attention. I didn't care for Mr Doig, but, my word, my marks shot up!

Mr Adamson was also a martinet, albeit a cheerful one, who when he took the register said 'Stand up all those who are absent.' On a wall in his room were the framed words 'YOUR BEST IS SUCCESS'.

Mr Burnett was of the age when he didn't do any physical jerks himself. Because he had been in India with the Army, he frequently had us marching round the gym while he called out 'Ek, do, tin, car (one, two, three, four in Hindustani)'.

Miss Guild, a tall, good-looking woman, terrified me so that I could get nothing right. One day, after I had broken some glass container, she said, 'Is there anything else you can do wrong, Malcolm?' And she was never slow to use the belt.

Mr Kitto was much more genial, and I got on better with him. However, as depute head, one of his duties was dealing with all boys who came late to school. On the single occasion when I was late, no reasons were asked for and he belted the lot. Eric, however, had a different experience. Kitto did ask for reasons, and the two boys in front of him proffered the feeble excuses of 'Alarm didn't go off' and 'Slept in'. He then turned to Eric, and when he said 'No excuse,' Kitto told him to go before punishing the other two.

Miss Martin, known as 'Granny Mertin', was another martinet who taught us little more than names and dates. Although I did next to no work at home, I did study for one of her exams the night before. This got me 90 per cent, but, when handing me the paper, she spoiled the moment by saying, 'I don't know how you did it, Malcolm.' Delighted, however, with the result, I rushed home to tell my mother, but thought I'd have a bit of fun first and told her I was sitting in the front row at history. This brought on a tirade which made me regret my folly, but Mother was placated when I explained that I had chosen to sit in front in order to see the blackboard.

Mr Cluckie must have dictated a lot of notes, because I still have a jotter filled with geographical information far beyond pupils of thirteen.

Miss Yeaman is primarily remembered because she sat on a desk in front of the class with her legs apart so that we saw her bloomers!

In 1938, I went on a school trip to Somerset. We left by special train from the Tay Bridge Station at 8.20 p.m. on 10 June, and arrived at the private siding of Fry, the chocolate company, in Keynsham, at 9.25 the next morning. After a tour of their Somerdale factory, we visited Wells Cathedral and Cheddar Gorge, by coach, and ended the day with a tour of Bristol before beginning the return, overnight, rail journey to Dundee. I still have the rail ticket issued by the LNER. Headed 'PARTY', it indicates that payment to them covered the whole trip, as the itinerary, including entrance to Gough's caves, is shown in detail. The booklet, produced by the school and indicating that 'Dr Kidd and Nurse' would accompany us, provided information about the places, together with a list headed 'What The Doctor Has To Say.' This included advice such as 'Do not stuff yourself with sweets' and 'Make up your mind to get as much sleep as you can', which was, of course, completely ignored. The train had a corridor with individual compartments, and I found it impossible to sleep in the overhead, cord, luggage rack! Light suppers and breakfasts were served, in two sittings, on both outward and return journeys, and Fry's provided lunch and tea.

Although lacking sleep, we enjoyed the trip immensely. The women in the factory wanted to touch my kilt for luck, and on leaving, we were each presented with a gilt box containing a selection of chocolate bars such as 'Five Boys'. Jimmy Begg was in the party, as were Alice and David Durie, and his older brother, Bob, came up from Bristol to meet us at Cheddar Gorge. I believe Mr Johnston (science) was one of the teachers in charge.

As the sight of an aeroplane in flight was uncommon in 1938, we looked up with mild interest when we heard one. This, however, was nothing to the excitement generated by seeing a plane with a smaller one on top of it, when about to enter school for an afternoon session. They flew quite low over the school and were seaplanes of Imperial Airways designed to capture the long-distance record.

Another reminiscence of Logie is of a red police-box being installed at its railings, on Blackness Road. These boxes, about the size of a telephone kiosk, had a small hinged door, behind which was a grill into which you spoke to police headquarters. As this was an innovation, we were asked to try it. This led to a mob at the box, although nobody had anything much to say.

I have a shadowy recollection of seeing Logie School being built as it opened in 1929 when I was four. It closed in 1975 and the building was given to the Harris Academy, by then a comprehensive, which used it for 1st- and 2nd-year classes. Harris vacated it in 1998, and it was demolished in 2002. Unknown to me when I was young, the Poorhouse of Liff and Benvie had previously stood on the site and the paupers had been transferred to the Eastern Poorhouse when the army requisitioned the building in 1914, renaming it the Western Barracks. It was then occupied by, firstly, the Black Watch, and later by the Argyll and Sutherland Highlanders, but although the latter vacated it in 1915, it remained unused until demolished for the construction of the school.

In June 1939, I obtained the Day School Certificate (Lower), but world events dictated that I was not to return to full-time study at the school after the summer holidays. When we holidayed in Llandudno that summer, attempts were being made to raise the brand-new submarine, HMS *Thetis*, which had failed to resurface from her first trial dive in Liverpool Bay.

15 Evacuation

I do not remember the summer of 1939 as regards the weather. I am told that it was a good one, but anyone who was old enough at the time, or who has made even a cursory study of twentieth-century history, knows that Hitler was on the rampage. I do remember that instead of returning to Logie Central School at the end of the summer holidays, I, along with my brother Eric and many others assembled in the playground of Blackness Public School, which Eric attended, and became 'evacuees'. Under the care of teachers, we were bid farewell by parents and friends and transported by rail to, what was to us children, an 'unknown destination'. I was fourteen years old and Eric was ten. I do not remember any tearful farewells; my father had to go to work in the Caledon shipyard as usual that day, but no doubt many children were frightened and all parents had heavy hearts.

My next recollection is of being in a very crowded school in the village of St Cyrus in Kincardineshire. Local people were being asked to take us 'poor' town kids into their homes, and I had a vague feeling of being up for auction. A kindly farmer's wife elected to take not only my brother and me but also another boy, Arthur Kettles, slightly younger than I, and his sister, Jessie, who could not have been more than seven.

Life at Milton of Mathers farm, by the sea and to the north of St Cyrus, was very pleasant. We were well cared for by Mrs Milne, the farmer's wife, and there were so many children based round the local primary school that lessons consisted mainly of rambles in the open air with a teacher, and the schoolwork which I had known became nonexistent. Then, one day, May, the only child of the farmer and his wife and a blond-haired lively girl of about my own age, returned from her studies at Montrose Academy to inform us that all evacuees of secondary school age were to go to her school, and so my life of almost complete leisure came to an end.

Montrose Academy then catered for the 'more able' children, and the education authority in Dundee had already decided that I was not one of this élite group as I had attended what was shortly to be called a junior secondary school. This meant that there was no hope of me attaining the higher reaches of education and entering a profession. In Dundee, I had been following a 'commercial' course, which meant that I was being trained to do routine office work. In Montrose Academy, only girls received such training, and because I had reached the advanced age of fourteen and had 'proceeded so far' with my training, the rector (my school in Dundee had a mere headmaster at the helm!) advised me to join a girls' class. I balked at this, but succumbed to his persuasive and reasoned argument, so I became the only boy in a class of girls.

Strange as it may seem, I found that I was not unhappy in this situation, although I felt obliged to retaliate when May and others made fun of it! It was infinitely preferable to being an appendage to a class of boys in a mathematics class, when a hard-faced lady teacher, on finding that I knew nothing of what the class was doing, held me up for ridicule by asking what they taught at the Dundee school I had attended.

In Dundee, our dinner break (nobody spoke of lunch in those days) had been from 12 noon until 1.15 p.m., but at Montrose the morning session lasted until 1 p.m. I found the hour between twelve and one agonizing, as I was always so hungry that I could pay but scant attention during this period. For the first time in my life I took school dinners. I remember nothing of the quality of these meals, but the quantity was sufficient, and that was what mattered to me. They were served by girl pupils, and there were always second helpings. I was impressed by the Latin grace which preceded the meals and which was said by a senior pupil. This established in my mind that I had indeed entered a seat of learning!

Life as an evacuee was going well when Eric and I suddenly lost our first home in the Mearns and were transferred to Hill of Morphie, a less opulent farm, to the west of the village. The transfer came as a shock, and I felt sad that Mrs Milne had got rid of us, although retaining her other two 'guests'. In retrospect, I realise that the work of caring for five children, including her own daughter, was too much for her and, quite naturally, little Jessie had captured her sympathy.

Although in a somewhat rougher and less well-off situation, Eric and I settled in quite well. We were, I am sure, just as well fed and housed, although Mrs Anderson, our new 'mother', had a great many people to look after. The farm was smaller than the first one and run entirely by the family. There were two sons, not long left school, a daughter of about thirteen and a boy of about eight. An older daughter, a nurse, was already away from home, but visited occasionally.

We got on well with everybody except Peter, the baby of the family, who was spoiled and whose violent tantrums were condoned. On one occasion, he threw an axe at Eric! The only toilet was outside, but, as it was never used, had become the habitat of roosting hens. It was the accepted thing that everybody used the steading. This came as somewhat of a shock to us, but we were very adaptable.

Eric now had to walk two miles to St Cyrus Primary School and had to carry sandwiches for his dinner. I had to walk about a mile, through fields, down to the main road, where I waited for the school bus which conveyed us 'country' children into Montrose.

We arrived in the Mearns in time for the grain harvest, and I remember the excitement among the children when the men worked in the evening to finish one particular field. As the tractor went round the field reducing the standing rectangle of corn with every circuit, rabbits, hares and field mice, which had lived within the crop, made a bid for freedom as their homes were demolished. The poor creatures were then chased by dogs and children armed with sticks. I doubt very much if any were caught, and certainly field mice, at least, would never have been harmed by us. But we thought it all great fun.

When autumn came, I had a holiday from school to help with the potato harvest. This was my one and only experience of 'tattie picking', and I went to work for six shillings (30p) a day at the adjacent and much larger Morphie farm owned by another family called Anderson. The family we lived with lent me overalls and heavy 'tackety' boots, and after a plate of porridge which was so full that the milk had to be spooned from a separate bowl, I set off to labour on frosty mornings, when keeping my hands warm was a major problem.

The tractor-drawn digger went round and round the field at what was to me a back-breaking pace. Until I got used to it, I found it almost impossible to gather all the potatoes in my 'bit', my pegged length of territory, into baskets before the machine came round again, and I had another crop to gather. During this critical period, when I was feeling a bit sorry for myself, a local lass came to my aid. She had the 'bit' adjacent to and ahead of mine, and, as soon as she had all her potatoes in baskets, she turned to help me. I have never forgotten her kindness. She didn't ask if I needed help but saw that I did.

As the sun rose each day, fingers thawed out. Gradually, over the passing days, the back became less sore as it became accustomed to the incessant bending. But some of my colleague 'tattie pickers' must have found the work too strenuous, because the labour force was reduced and the farmer made the 'bits' longer, while the tractor-digger maintained the same unrelenting pace. This proved too much for the town children who were left and eventually we were worked so hard that a 'strike' ensued.

I remember a group of us gathering crab apples in nearby Den o' Morphie when the grieve caught up with us. After much futile cursing, he begged us to return to work with the promise that the tractor would travel more slowly and that our temporary departure would be overlooked. We readily agreed, but, when I had returned to Dundee some time later and received my wages by cheque, I was not paid for that day. My father wrote to the farmer about this, but received no satisfaction. Together with many others, I worked for something like seven hours that day without payment. My objective had been to provide Eric with a bike so that he could cycle to the village school.

As the nights 'drew in', we spent the evenings playing a card game called 'Please and Thank You', which I had never heard of before and have never heard of since. It is no doubt one of those simple games which give a lot of fun. All I remember of it is that when you ask another player for a card you have to say 'please' and when you get it you have to say 'thank you'. It was at least a good way of teaching manners.

I spent one day working with Mr Anderson, our adoptive father, and his two older sons. The job was spreading dung which had been deposited in regular heaps across a field. We began together at the bottom of the field, and, each armed with a fork, threw the dung over the ground. I was young with plenty of energy, but, in no time at all, the others were away ahead of me as each kept to his own row of heaps. I was very sensitive that the others were laughing at my efforts to keep up with them, but soon they were a long way off and I was left struggling on my own. It was a humiliating experience, but one which taught me that the work of a farm labourer is generally undervalued and that most of us cannot do it.

Mr Anderson was a stockily built man of about fifty who sported a large moustache. He never had much to say, but was held in high regard by his hard-working wife and family. When sitting in his chair during the evenings, he would noisily and deliberately 'break wind' at which all the family would laugh. When his wife baked pancakes, as she always did, he would spread one with butter and jam and then slap another on top with a grand gesture. We all followed his example regarding the pancakes. No one ever took only one.

My mother had visited us when we were resident at the Milton of Mathers. I remember her visit because she was standing at the end of the road leading to the farm and caught me chasing May off the school bus – May having been goading me about my membership of the girls' class! Now both parents came to see how we were faring in our second abode. They found that we were fitting in what they considered to be too well in our new 'rough' environment, so they decided to take us home, especially as Dundee had not received and never did receive much attention from the Germans. And so ended, somewhat abruptly, our sojourn in the Mearns.

POSTSCRIPT In 1993, Eric and I went to see where we had been evacuated to. The small Hill of Morphie farm had been incorporated into the larger Morphie farm, and the farmhouse was occupied by an oil worker and his wife and small daughter. They made us welcome and showed us round the house, but had no knowledge of the Andersons who had taken us into their home over half a century earlier and who had worked so hard to maintain their farm.

16 My Working Life Begins

Our return to Dundee began an almost completely new life for me as I was no longer a schoolboy but on the threshold of my working life. As I had been trained for office work at school, I began scanning the 'situations vacant' columns of the *Dundee Courier and Advertiser* and applied for jobs labelled either 'office boy' or 'apprentice clerk'.

I had interviews for three jobs: two in jute offices and the other in the office of an engineering firm. The gentleman who interviewed me for the last position insisted that, after a brief term as office boy, I should become an apprentice engineer. However I steadfastly declined this opportunity, because I had no wish to become an engineer. He did his best to persuade me, but, having failed, asked what my father did for a living. We both smiled when I replied that my father was an engineer!

One of the other interviews was for a job in a very small jute office where I was set a written arithmetic examination by an equally small, portly and bald-headed gentleman. I took the exam seriously, but knew, even as I sat it, that I was failing miserably. I have since learned that, according to Socrates, a knowledge of one's ignorance is the beginning of wisdom and take comfort in this. I certainly failed that examination and pity the poor innocent who passed!

My successful interview was for the position of office boy with A. & S. Henry & Co. Ltd, 60 Victoria Road, where I was interviewed by Mr G. Archbold, the amiable chartered accountant/secretary. He did not seem to mind that my school marks had been mediocre, and so I became an office boy. This meant that I came under the direct authority of Don Shaw, a kindly middle-aged spinster, and sat on a bench-seat in the small office of the uniformed and be-medalled commissionaire, just inside the main entrance and at the foot of the beautiful marble staircase, awaiting orders. I spent only three weeks as an office boy, but over three years as a clerk. During these years, I was extremely underpaid as, although not yet fifteen, I took over the job of a man of thirty who had gone to the Forces and who had been paid considerably more. But the firm allowed me almost complete freedom, as long as I did my job, and I was happy indeed in that situation.

My three weeks as office boy were great fun. There were three of us youngsters, and we took it in turn to race about the town on foot, delivering letters and parcels and, in general, running errands to businesses in the central area of the city. I visited places which had previously been unknown to me, and, although there was 'a war on', almost everyone I came in contact with was pleasant and cheerful. (The rhetorical question 'Don't you know there's a war on?' was in constant use when you asked for anything even slightly out of the ordinary or to be done in a hurry.)

I still remember some of the more unusual errands on which I was sent. One was to a barber's shop to have the managing director's open razor sharpened. This led me to believe that it was more dignified to shave with an 'open' rather than a 'safety' razor! (The electric razor was unknown to us at that time.) Then, as Christmas and New Year were approaching, I went to the office of Stewart's Cream of the Barley in Castle Street to collect a bottle of whisky for the head of a department. As this errand was outside the norm, I was told that I might take advantage of the privilege of purchasing a bottle of wine for my parents at thrupence (3d/1p) below the retail price. This information was conveyed to my 'teetotal' parents in great excitement, and they gratefully took advantage of it for 'first-foots' arriving at the New Year.

On one occasion, I was sent to deliver a letter to a subsidiary firm of the company, whose premises were over a mile away in the west end of the city, and was given thrupence for the return tram fare. As the tram route was a circuitous one through the city centre, I decided to sprint directly across to the West Port where I could catch a tram to my destination for only a hape-ny (half-penny/½d) and so make a penny for myself on both the outward and return journeys. But when I boarded a tram somewhat out of breath, I was thinking of something else and mistakenly asked for a three hape-ny (1½d) ticket. And, having issued the ticket, the conductor could do nothing about it. My sprint to earn a penny had been for nothing and it is amazing how a catastrophe of such magnitude remains in one's memory.

It would certainly not be Miss Shaw who gave me an envelope to deliver to Mr J. Carmichael, 1 Albert Square. I couldn't find the address and nobody I asked was any help as it was an old trick. The statue of James Carmichael stands in the square, as does that of Mr R. Burns!

Regarding Albert Square, I once exited the city

library when the man behind me spun the revolving door at a rate of knots. This caused a male librarian to rush out and collar me for the misdemeanour, but, after I'd pointed out the culprit, I left the two of them in heated argument.

Office boys were responsible for opening the mail in the morning, and we made a few extra pennies by looking out for stamps on letters which had not been franked. These stamps were carefully removed, stuck on to outgoing letters and the relevant amount taken from the petty cash! Carried in a large, leather, briefcase-type bag with the company's name emblazoned on it in gold letters, and with a shoulder strap attached, outgoing mail was taken to the GPO at the end of the day. Similarly occupied, many girls and boys converged on the GPO, in Ward Road, around 5.30 p.m.

After three weeks as an office boy, I began my apprenticeship to become a clerk, although no indentures were signed. The apprenticeship was for three years with a salary (not to be confused with a wage) of £30, £40 and £50 a year. I rushed home to tell my mother of my promotion. In only three weeks, I had risen from being an office boy, paid a 'wage' of 10s (50p) a week, less 4d (less than 2p) for an insurance stamp, to being an apprentice clerk earning a 'salary' of £30 a year and paid monthly! The increase was barely 2s (10p) a week, but it was not the additional bounty which mattered so much as the step up the ladder of success. The girls in the factory earned more, but my prospects were better, as in those days managing directors often began as office boys and apprentice clerks.

(During this early part of the war, the town schools remained closed, so many teachers held classes in their own homes. Invergowrie Primary, however, was still functioning, and Mother, who had once attended the school, managed to have Eric enrolled. He cycled the four miles there and back. After becoming friendly with Bruce Leith, he got his dinner at his home.)

17 The 'Top Flat'

My promotion took me to a part of the building which I had known only remotely. I was not in the main office, which must have had a staff of at least fifty, but in the small office of Victoria Road Calender, located in the sewing-machine flat of the factory on the top floor of the building. The main office was quiet and pleasant; here there was the incessant noise of sewing machines as jute bags were made.

All the machine operators were women, and each operator had a girl assistant whose job it was to do the labouring work of keeping the machinists supplied with jute cloth as well as 'hauling off' and folding the finished bags. Apart from the office staff, the only men employed on the 'top flat' were: two or three pairs of cutters whose job it was to cut the cloth to the required length according to the size of bags being made; a stamp cutter, who cut out rubber stamps and nailed them to rollers for marking the bags; his boss, who supervised the stamping operation; and a man who conveyed the finished bags to the shute, which carried them to the ground floor for dispatch.

Only three clerks, including me, worked in the 'top flat' office. The lower part of the office was made of wood and the upper part of glass, so that we had a view of the women working at the sewing machines. And as the noise of the machines was considerable, any noise we made could not be heard outside. We took advantage of this and, at the drop of a hat, used to bawl out such songs as 'Paper Moon' and 'It Was Only A Shanty In Old Shanty Town'. They were already old songs at the time, but favourites of David Scrimgeour, the 'boss'. Such outbursts were both loud and sporadic when the accompaniment and beat were provided by one of us running our fingers across the keys of the adding machine and the others rattling on the end of the desks with pen or pencil. We bawled to our hearts content and no one outside our small sanctuary was aware of the racket.

My job consisted of four main tasks, and, in spite of the fun, I had a lot of work to do. One task was to check all the 'time cards' of the workers who had to 'clock in'. They worked from 7.45 a.m. till noon and from 1 p.m. till 5.30 p.m. If they were more that three minutes late, morning or afternoon, they were 'quartered'.

This meant that I was required to record the lateness, and a quarter of an hour's pay was deducted. Although always conscientious, I was somewhat 'careless' if the tardiness were marginal.

Another job was to calculate the amount of work done by the cutters,* who were not permitted to begin cutting until one of us confirmed that their wooden mark was set at the correct length. On piece-work, they worked very hard indeed and earned £5 to £6 a week at a time when a tradesman's wage was about £3. I found these calculations an extremely onerous task because the wages department in the main office were always at me to produce the results in record time.

A third job was to write labels for all the bundles of bags for dispatch. This was simple enough, but everything was wanted in a hurry. Among the customers to whom I addressed labels were Spillers, Herdman and Rank.

Lastly, when all the pressing jobs had been done, I had to file away the paper patterns of the ink stamps placed on the bags for the various firms.

When I first took over the job, I always felt under pressure and found it very difficult to cope. Life became more bearable as expertise developed.

But what made the 'top flat' so interesting and enjoyable was that it was full of 'characters'. One of

---

* David Scrimgeour said that he didn't object to anyone swearing, but when McInally, one of the cutters, inserted an expletive into words such as Na—poleon, he thought this a bit much!

these was Annie Lamb, the lady in charge of all the women. She was in her fifties, wore small-framed, steel-rimmed glasses, was extremely neat in her brown overall and did her best to hide a kind heart under a brusque exterior. When she was around, none of the male office staff who came up from the main office was permitted to swear in my young and innocent presence, although she herself swore like a trooper. Needless to say, they took extreme delight in breaking this rule! She would curse the girls under her, but, if anyone else said a word against them, she turned on the offender with venom. The girls were her domain. She had the right to slander them but nobody else did, and if they did so it was at their peril. Jess Clunie, Annie's depute and second-in-charge, was the antithesis of her. A quiet girl in her twenties, Jess was a Jehovah's Witness whose brother had fought in the International Brigade during the Spanish Civil War.

Another of the 'characters' was Jock Dargie, who trundled the bales of jute bags from the sewing machines to the wooden shute by which they descended to the loading bay for dispatch. He was always in shirt-sleeves, wore a jute apron to protect his clothes and was never without his bonnet. A relic of an older generation, he always wore a waistcoat and boots and frequently chewed tobacco.

Youngsters like myself quickly learned that there was no love lost between Annie and Jock. If we saw Jock passing, we would often signal him into the office when he would soberly bring his barrow to a halt and enter our 'buckie' or small office. We would ask him, in a subdued confidential voice, what he thought of Annie. The reaction was always the same; he did not want to discuss such a distasteful subject. But it took very little coaxing to get him started! Somehow, as often as not when he was in the middle of his diatribe, Annie, to our great delight, would be seen heading for the office, but we encouraged Jock to continue until she burst through the door. With his back to the door, Annie's entrance came as a complete surprise and Jock's confusion was our delight which we endeavoured to heighten by such remarks as, 'Jock was just saying what a lot he thinks of you, Annie.' Annie would give an assumed off-hand 'Och aye', while Jock made a hasty excuse to depart. Somehow I doubt if the 'bad blood' between them was all that serious. At any rate, we liked them both.

When it was Annie's birthday, I was designated to go out to buy a leather pouffe for her. She surprised us by coming into the office when I was wrapping it up again after showing it to my colleagues. As her birthday was the next day, I told her it was a present for my mother, whereupon Annie examined it and expressed her opinion that it was a lovely gift. When it was given to her the following day, she didn't know what to say.

When I first began work in the 'top flat' office, I sat beside a tall, moustached and already balding youth in his twenties who was awaiting his 'call-up' into the

Forces. He was something of a scholar with an interest in politics, and I can remember how he expressed exaggerated surprise when I confessed to never having heard of the Tolpuddle Martyrs. He had obviously been better educated by the history department of Dundee High School than I had been by its counterpart at Logie Central. Lethargy was Gerry's middle name, and he would sit at ease with nothing to do while I, at fourteen years of age, felt under extreme pressure with cutters' calculations awaited urgently by the wages department, or with labels for bags awaiting immediate despatch. A few months after his 'call-up' into the Army, Gerry visited us with sergeant's stripes on his uniform. After the war, I heard that he had become a schoolteacher.

I arrived at work on the morning of 14 February 1940 to find a letter on my desk. This was a most unusual thing and I wondered who on earth could have written to me. My colleagues gathered round as I opened it, and lo and behold, to my surprise and embarrassment, it was a Valentine card. I was very shy of girls and wondered who could possibly have sent the card. But *they* all knew and my reaction, and their subsequent comments, must have justified their efforts!

In spite of the volume of work, there was a great deal of larking about. One day when I saw John Bruce, the young lad who had replaced Gerry, returning to the office, I got down behind the door and prevented his entrance. He couldn't see me because I was behind the wooden part, but, knowing I was there, put his shoulder to the door and came right through the glass panel. This took the shine off the prank, but when John reported the 'accident' without naming the real culprit to Mr Strachan, the works' manager, he got off with a swearing. John was a phlegmatic and pleasant lad and apparently highly regarded by some of the works' girls so that they scribbled his name on the wall of their toilet. It was Annie who passed on this information, and, when she was arguing with John after that, she would call him 'a shit-house hero'!

I think it was John who sold me what was obviously a counterfeit 2s (10p) piece for thrupence. Although I had some qualms about using it, I entered a trick shop in the Overgate and bought a fake packet of cigarettes. My guilt somewhat disappeared when, on saying that it wasn't much of a trick, the male assistant replied 'What do you expect for thrupence?' and a considerable profit was made.

The works' electrician was Mr Mackay – a pleasant enough man who wore a brown boiler suit and, although indoors, a cap. (Mr Strachan also wore a cap, but his status was displayed by his white overall.) Mr Mackay, in his fifties, had a superior air about him, so that, behind his back, he was referred to as 'Count' Mackay. Always interested in seeing another aspect of the work which went on in the large building, I accompanied Mr Mackay to the boiler room one day. He was carrying a cardboard box full of electric bulbs and asked me to hold the box 'for a minute'. I reached out for the box, but it crashed to the floor before I got hold of it and the bulbs were shattered. I was naturally alarmed. I thought it was my mistake, but Mr Mackay was laughing. They were old bulbs and he had done it deliberately. But there was a day when Mr Mackay was not laughing: his son, serving in Bomber Command, had been posted 'missing' and was never to return.

Another young lad who worked beside me for a time was Alistair Marnie, the blond son of a butcher in Arthurstone Terrace. When I was staying with my grandparents (sleeping in a feather bed), because my parents and Eric were on holiday, I went out for a run on my bike one Sunday and met Alistair and a pal near Morgan Academy. They were setting out to return a young snipe to where they had found it somewhere north of Dundee. I joined up with them, and on the way Alistair took the bird out of its box and put it on the saddle of his bike as his pushed it through Lumley Den. The small bird fell off and, much to our distress, was killed. We continued towards Glen Isla, and, as it was getting late, the other lad decided he'd had enough and went home.

It was a lovely summer's day, and Alistair and I made up our minds to go right through Glen Isla and return home by Alyth and Meigle. It was seven o'clock when we were in the Glen, with the river Isla at some distance below us. Although we had carried no swimming gear, we decided to go for a swim and parked our bikes just over the wire fence at the side of the road. After the swim, we continued into Glen Isla village and it was there that I discovered that my pump was missing and surmised that I had lost it at the spot where we had gone swimming. We returned and found the pump.

As time was now worrying us, there was nothing for it but to return to Dundee the way we had come. As we headed home, the miles became harder to cover and we were making heavy weather of it as we cycled the long climb up Glen Ogilvie. It was already dark and we were well up the glen when a lorry, heading in the opposite direction, stopped and the driver asked us if we had seen two fellows on bikes. We said we hadn't and the driver continued on his way.

We had negotiated Glen Ogilvie and Lumley Den and were in the region of Tealing when a lorry, heading in the same direction, passed us and stopped. It was the same man who had asked us about the two missing cyclists. 'Would you like a lift?' he asked. Never in my life have I been more grateful for a lift. Our bikes were put onto the back of the lorry, and we travelled in the cabin with the driver. He dropped us somewhere in the east end of the city so that, as I lived in the west end, I cycled through the deserted streets and I was home by 1 a.m. It was a marvellous and memorable day with the only blight being the concern that I had given my grandparents, who had anxiously waited up for me.

On answering the phone one day, the caller was Willie Miller, in the main office, asking for David

Scrimgeour. When I replied 'He's just went out,' Willie corrected me by saying 'He's just gone out.' I never made that mistake again. Willie went to sea as a radio officer and was third R/O on the Anglo-Saxon tanker *Conus*, when, sailing independently and bound for Curaçao, she was torpedoed and sunk on 4 April 1941. And, as all fifty-nine on board lost their lives, her fate remained unknown until disclosed by the German navy after the war.

The works' entrance was in the narrow lane to the east of the building, and there was a watchman permanently on the door. He was an elderly man who did not generally have anything to say to me, but there was one memorable day in June 1941 when he did. Obviously excited, he had to impart the news to somebody. 'Russia's in the war,' he blurted out. 'On whose side?' I asked.

After over a year in the 'top flat' office, I asked for and was granted a transfer to the main office which was situated several floors below and far removed from the noise of sewing machines. I told the company secretary that I wanted more experience, but this was only partly true. I also wanted another hour in bed in the morning and felt that I had started at 8 a.m. for long enough when those in the general office began at 9 a.m. for the same money. They also had an hour and a half for dinner, whereas the 'top flat' office had an hour and a quarter, and, in most cases, juniors carried a much lighter burden.

It is almost unbelievable today that clerks employed by the same company and working in the same building would work seven and a quarter more hours per week without extra payment. This amounted to almost an extra day's work every week, yet it was considered bad taste even to mention it. Not only that, but I always felt that those who did the longer hours were regarded as being slightly inferior to those who mounted the marble staircase to the main office!

My transfer to the main office gave me not only another hour in bed but also saved me from pedalling my poorly lit bike in the blackout through the crowds of women heading for the jute mills on dark winter mornings, when some of them vociferously expressed their opinion of my steering!

18 The General Office

Although no cotton bags were produced in the building, I now became the junior clerk in the cotton department, where Mr Ferrier, a small, reticent, greying man in his fifties, was the boss. His sole assistant was David Cathro, who already wore the RAFVR lapel badge, and I had come to replace him when he left for the RAF. David was clever and efficient and, as he did not try to cultivate popularity, was regarded by some as a snob, although I did not find him so. We became and remained good friends for many years, and he eventually became managing director.

The general or main office was a pleasant environment in which to work. It was designed, to some extent, on what later became known as the open-plan system as only glass partitions separated most of the departments. This meant that your activities could be seen by everybody, but the 'atmosphere' was good and, provided you did your job, nobody bothered you. It was an 'atmosphere' of responsible freedom, which nobody seriously abused.

Dress was formal. All the men wore suits to work, and the seniors – and particularly the heads of departments – displayed their seniority by also wearing bowler hats. Saturday morning, however, was different. Sportswear was permitted, and the seniors who were playing golf in the afternoon appeared in plus-fours and cloth caps. I wore shorts until I was sixteen, and, to begin with, wore my first suit with long trousers only on a Sunday.

My job required me to cost orders for cotton bags. Using simple arithmetic, I had to work out how much the firm was to charge a customer for a given number of bags of a given size and quality. The cost of transport by rail (goods were mainly transported by rail in those days) was added to the cost of material and labour, plus a margin of profit for the company. A letter was then sent to the prospective buyer informing him of the cost of the intended purchase. This letter was dictated by me to a shorthand typist who was often summoned to my desk from the typing pool by a junior of fourteen years of age. He would be sent by me (aged sixteen or seventeen) to obtain a typist and would enter the typing pool, asking the head typist for a 'typist for Mr Malcolm, please'. The shorthand typist would arrive. I would give her my high stool and would stand dictating the letter. I felt rather proud of this situation to begin with, but it soon became routine and nobody thought anything of the fact that a mere youth did this work and accepted the responsibility of a man.

In my recollection, apart from the managing director's secretary and the lady on the switchboard, women worked only in the typing pool and the invoice room. All the departments consisted, usually, of only two men. The one that impressed me was the foreign department. A great deal of their business was with South America, and Mr Hardie, in his forties and with a superior air about him, dictated letters in Spanish to two shorthand typists who were also proficient in the language. During my time as an office boy, I forgot to send a telegram of his which was to Finland. I discovered it in my pocket during the evening, was immediately in a panic, and sent it off before arriving at work the next morning. But, perhaps unnecessarily, I confessed that I had failed to send it off from the GPO the previous evening and was made to feel that I had committed a serious crime. Incidentally, the lady on the switchboard must have lived in the country, as she occasionally had me deliver half a dozen eggs to friends of hers who lived near me and I was given one for my trouble.

There were no tea or coffee breaks in these days, but there was a recognised break in the forenoon when a number of us, including some who were not 'juniors', descended the stairs to the beautifully tiled men's washroom, where we formed a circle and kept a shuttlecock in the air using only our feet.

When the Germans carried out air raids on British cities they would set them ablaze by dropping great numbers of incendiary bombs. People throughout the country therefore did 'fire-watching' duty in order to extinguish fires with stirrup pumps before the fires got a hold. In our office, I think it was only the men (anyone male over fourteen) who were asked to volunteer, and throughout my years with the firm I certainly performed this duty only with men. We were given the scantiest of training. On one occasion only, I was sent to Dudhope Park where I donned a boiler suit and gas mask and crawled into a small brick construction with a stirrup pump to put out a small, smouldering fire. That was the sum total of my training. Every night, four or five of us 'defended' our massive jute complex – a potential inferno!

I was on duty about every tenth night. I enjoyed these nights spent in the huge deserted building when we played cards late into the night and slept on camp beds. We were not paid for 'fire-watching', but received a subsistence allowance, which may have amounted to 3s 6d (17½p); certainly it was no more than this, and more likely it was less. One of those with whom I regularly fire-watched was Mr Tulloch, a Jewish gentleman in his fifties who knew several languages but was especially proud of the fact that we all appreciated the excellent porridge which he made, using milk instead of water, for our breakfast. Although 'fire-watching' was a voluntary activity, I suspect that pressure was put on the older men. I cannot remember if any heads of departments volunteered, but Mr Caldwell, the managing director, certainly did not fire-watch. At around two o'clock one morning, Joe Macfarlane, who was a year or so older than me, hit upon the idea of rousing the MD from his slumbers. I stood beside him while he made the phone call and quietly returned the phone to its rest when the call was answered! Although I regularly saw Mr Caldwell – a tall, grey-haired and austere man of about sixty – I don't think he ever addressed a word to me. Incidentally, only the better-off had phones in their homes, and I don't think I ever used the phone until I was working. When my family wanted to make a call, we used the red, wooden telephone boxes, where the A button was pressed to allow your tuppence to fall into the metal receptacle when the call was answered, or the B button was pressed to return your money if it were not. The B button was always pressed after a call – just in case there was some money left over!

I always went home for my dinner. The distance was about one and a half miles, and, as we had an hour and a half, I walked or cycled. When I needed a haircut, I usually went, at dinner time, to a barber shop in Blackness Road, which was located roughly where the fire station is now, near the top of Forest Park Road. Because the barber shop was always referred to as Rossie's, I thought that the barber's name was Rossi and that he was of Italian extraction. But Dundonians have a great habit of using the diminutive, and the barber's name was Ross. With Blackness Foundry close by, Rossie's was a thriving business and Mr Ross employed three other barbers. The shop was particularly busy on a Friday evening when all the chairs were occupied and men from the foundry sat waiting, on the long bench, to have a haircut or a shave, or both. Listening to the good-humoured repartee made waiting more of an entertainment than a chore.

19 Life Outside the Office

During the winter months, work for many youngsters did not end at 5.30 p.m. as we attended night school/evening classes from 7 p.m. till 9 p.m. Perhaps some attended these classes because they really wanted to, but the vast majority felt the often unspoken compulsion of parents coupled with a vague notion that the acquisition of further plebeian certificates might lead to better things. I attended night classes in my old school over a period of three winters, studying English, arithmetic, shorthand, typewriting and bookkeeping. Most of us hated it, and I certainly did. I used to view the approach of the night school winter with a kind of foreboding, and pleasant days at work were overshadowed by the prospect of yet another evening at night school. Previous generations of youngsters had been compelled to suffer long hours of manual labour, but many of my generation worked long hours by what appeared to be our own volition. Strangely enough, the evening classes themselves were not all bad. My teachers, all of whom I had had at day school, were kindly enough people who did their best for their pupils. I am sure that we profited intellectually from their instruction, but there was no extra remuneration for certificates gained at night school. Many of today's youngsters complain of a lack of amenities so that 'there is nothing to do' and they are bored. But would they want things organised for them as they were for us? I have known some complain of being 'compelled' to spend one day of their working week at a college on day-release – a whole day every week studying at the employer's expense! Perhaps I would feel the same in their shoes, as it seems to be human nature never to appreciate what is too easily available. Today's evening classes are largely the preserve of the middle class endeavouring to arrange flowers, keep fit, service their cars or improve their golf. During one of these wartime classes, the teacher announced that a company of the Army cadet force was being formed and added the carrot that any who volunteered would be given sergeants' stripes. Nobody volunteered.

My Day School Certificate (Lower) bears the rubber-stamp signature of John L. Peters, the headmaster when I had been a full-time pupil, but the Junior Secondary Certificate, which I qualified for in 1940, bears the personal signature of A.C. Mackenzie who had succeeded him.

During the first year of the war, I also attended the Friday night sessions of the Former Pupils' Association (annual subscription 1s 6d/7½p*), where we played games and learned country dancing under the excellent instruction of Miss Reid, the girls' gym teacher. When the electric period bell rang to indicate that the dancing was about to commence, almost everyone headed for the hall. Miss Reid, standing on the stage, demonstrated the steps. Having learned the correct ones, I could never after be bothered with dancers who just went in for birling and hooching!

When I eventually left Logie after these early war years at night school, I little thought that I would

---

* The light green membership card sported a drawing of the clock and wind vane on the roof of the school, together with the School motto 'Nitendo Gaudemus' ('In Flourishing We Rejoice').

have any contact with the school again. But when I was in my year of teacher training at Moray House, in Edinburgh, directors of education from the various authorities came to recruit teachers. When I saw the Dundee director, I asked for a post at Logie. His reply was that teachers were engaged to serve the education authority and not a particular school, but when I insisted he gave me Logie.

Due to a housing problem, I spent only the autumn term of 1961 at the school. In some ways, it was the same, and Mr Smith, now depute head, Miss Ness, Miss M. Clark and Miss Reid were still in harness. The classes were still lined up in the two inner rectangles (one for boys and one for girls) with a teacher calling them to attention, plus an instruction to stretch out their arms to make space between pairs before they marched into school. Previously, classes had been of mixed sex. Now, however, boys and girls were kept separate, and there was a dining hall and a sports' field, at Elliot Road. Also, due to the leaving age being raised to fifteen and the consequent increase in numbers, Dudhope School had been acquired as an annex. A new departure, too, was that during a morning period two pupils from every class were sent to collect a crate of milk. This came in one-third-of-a-pint bottles, issued free, and was drunk through straws, at the desks. In my days as a pupil, the same quantity of milk was available for a half-penny. Incidentally, the boys used to jump on to the sides of the milk lorry as it entered the Glenagnes entrance to the playground. When Eric was a pupil, a boy doing this fell under the wheels and was killed.

I particularly remember a senior class which I had for English: a bright set of fifteen-year-old girls who, if they had been born later, would have qualified for an 'O' Grade and more. It was Christmas time when I was leaving, and they presented me with a pair of leather gloves, which I still have. I had not disclosed to them that I had been a pupil at the school and, when thanking them for the gloves, I made this known. Much to my surprise, they all shouted out, 'We know, Mr Peden [the headmaster] told us.' It was a moment to be remembered and, when I saw them all singing at the Christmas Service in St John's Cross Church, I felt quite emotional.

Other pupils and incidents also come to mind. A small girl, called Margaret, was going round the classes saying goodbye to her teachers on her last day at school. Margaret had been a source of annoyance at times and, well aware of this, she said to me, 'Ye'll hae meh wee sister next year, but she no gie ye ony trouble. She goes tae church carrying her bible.' But although she had put up a front of not liking school, the moment was too much for her and she burst into tears. I liked Margaret.

I think that it was Margaret's class that informed me one morning that one of their number had swallowed a needle the previous evening. On questioning the girl, she confirmed that this was indeed the case, and when

I asked if her parents knew, she said that they did and said to wait and see what would happen! I sent for Miss Beveridge, the Lady Superintendent, and, after further questioning, the girl was dispatched to hospital. The needle was seen under x-ray, but I cannot recall how it was removed.

All teachers were required to teach Bible Studies, and, not being religious, I wasn't sure how to go about it with a class of non-certificate boys which contained one of the most troublesome boys in the school. In the end, it didn't prove to be a problem. They sat engrossed as I read the story of Exodus, and when that ended, I held discussions on moral issues which I had to arbitrarily bring to a halt some time after the 4 o'clock bell had signified the end of the school day.

Then there was the day when boys were playing football when I was crossing the inner quadrangle, going from the dining hall to my classroom. They did not discontinue their game as I passed and, when the ball hit me hard in the square of the back, I collared the culprit and told him to come to my room, where I gave him two of the belt. But, like the teacher in Invergowrie, that boy was a psychologist as, on leaving the room, he turned and said, 'I'm sorry I hit you, sir.'

I learned to type not at Logie night school but at Foley's College in the Murraygate, which was run by the diminutive Mr Foley and which was located approximately above Woolworth's and where Tesco now is. I do not remember why I went there in preference to the cheaper state school, but my parents paid Mr Foley's modest fees. I was fifteen when he taught me to touch-type, and, as I have used this skill ever since, I have good reason to be grateful to him. I remember his college for two other reasons. One is that he noticed that I was plagued with warts on my fingers and asked if I had ever heard of Emile Coué. I had not. He then told me of Coué's belief in 'auto-suggestion' and to plant a piece of beef in the earth, whereupon my warts would disappear. I absorbed what he told me, but felt that my parents and everyone else would laugh at this. I told nobody, but, when alone, planted a small piece of raw meat from some I found in the house – and my warts did disappear.

My other recollection of Foley's College is that of a dark winter evening and the dismal fluctuating wail of the air-raid sirens. Mr Foley then asked if we had previously heard sounds which might have been explosions, but nobody else had heard anything. I walked home and when I reached the top of Rosefield Street on my way up Blackness Road, there were many people about as a bomb had demolished the tenement at 19 Rosefield Street. I began to feel some anxiety for my own home, and it turned out that our windows had been broken and a ceiling cracked by another bomb which had fallen behind the tenement across the road.

This was the night of 5 November 1940. Most of the occupants of the Rosefield Street tenement had most fortunately chosen to go out that evening, but two people were killed. One was Mary Ann Laing, aged sixty-four, who lived in the building, while the other was Robert Cairns Coventry, aged sixty-six, who had chosen to visit his friend that evening from his home in Beechwood. Nobody was killed or injured by the other bomb, which had succeeded in demolishing only a washhouse.

On another night when the sirens sounded, I went with my family to Mr and Mrs Mollison's house on the first floor of our tenement, for safety. We all sat listening to the dreadful drone of German bombers as they passed over in waves. Not a bomb was dropped on Dundee, but the experience was terrifying. In the morning, we learned that Clydebank had been the target. Clydebank was bombed on the two consecutive nights of 13 and 14 March 1941. If our experience was terrifying, what must it have been like in Clydebank, where more than twelve hundred people were killed, thousands more injured and almost every house destroyed or damaged so that the majority were made homeless. But almost all wartime films and literature state that it was England – and not Britain – which was at war. When 'There will always be an England' was played, many Scots sang an alternative version which went '. . . as long as Scotland's here and little Wales is by her side and Ireland (Ulster) over there'.

Life, however, was not all work, and the wireless (then the exclusive province of the BBC and not referred to as the 'radio' in that pre-television era) was very important to us. At the beginning of the war, I often went to John Duncan's house to play 'Monopoly'. One evening, his father made us stop shaking the dice while Churchill made – what may have been – his 'We shall fight on the beaches' broadcast. The gravity of the situation was lost on us. We were anxious to get on with the game.

During the early war years, we listened to Lord Haw-Haw broadcasting in English. He began with 'Germany calling. Germany calling.' Lord Haw-Haw, the nickname given to William Joyce, was listened to with some amusement and not a little trepidation. We knew he told lies, but also that he recounted losses which the British government did not wish to have highlighted or even disclosed. Most of us eventually gave up listening to Joyce, who was an Irish-American. He made his last broadcast on 30 April 1945, the day Hitler committed suicide. Very drunk and speaking from a Hamburg in ruins, his last words were 'You may not hear from me again for a few months. Es lebe Deutschland. Heil Hitler and farewell.' In 1946, he was convicted of treason and hanged, because he was considered to be British although the passport which he held had been illegally obtained.

Then there were the grave items which sometimes preceded the BBC's nine o'clock (p.m.) news, when the announcer read the sinister words 'The Admiralty regret to announce the loss of HMS ——.' In early February 1943, the ship concerned was HMS *Erica*, on board which was young Joe Begg. Happily, Joe survived, but

I remember the distress of my mother when she heard the announcement, and her exclamation 'That's Joe's ship.' No such announcements were made regarding merchant ships – their losses were all too many.

But the BBC helped keep our spirits up. The whole of Britain tuned in to the weekly broadcasts of Tommy Handley's ITMA (*It's That Man Again*) and we laughed at Arthur Askey's *Band Wagon* and, according to his 'radio wife', the 'useless' Rob Wilton who began his act by saying 'The day war broke out, my missus said to me, what good are ye?' And this was the era of the big bands such as Joe Loss, Billy Cotton, Victor Silvester, Glen Miller and Tommy Dorsey, whose styles were immediately recognised by the younger generation.

A great deal of my spare time was spent with the 3rd Dundee (YMCA) Company of the Boys' Brigade, which met in the YMCA building near the bottom of Constitution Road. There were times when I spent almost every evening of the week at the BB, and this was indeed time well spent. Due to the fear of night raids at the beginning of the war, it was thought unwise to congregate on the traditional Friday evening, so that we met on Sunday, but, as time went on, the Friday meeting was restored.

The evening's activities began with an hour of drill. Most of today's youngsters resent regimentation, and my father, who had drilled with a rifle in the 4th (St Marks, Perth Road) Company before the First World War, considered that the BB had trained his generation for war. (He was, nevertheless, always nostalgic about both the BB and the Army!) An hour of drill is hard work, but it made us smart and alert. We took part in drill competitions against other BB companies, and few of us ever walked about with our hands in our pockets – a practice which my father wouldn't allow anyway.

After the hour of drill, we engaged in various educational activities such as signalling* and first aid. When we passed the various tests, we were awarded badges which we proudly displayed on our right arms, near the shoulder, when on special parade. I attended the BB swimming club on Monday evenings, pipe band practice on Thursdays, Bible class on Sunday mornings and played football for the company on Saturday afternoons. Perhaps we were the only Dundee company which, win or lose, gave three cheers for our opponents after every game.

The BB taught me a great deal that school did not, such as how to keep the sheepskin bag of the pipes supple. This was done by disconnecting it and pouring treacle into it. It was then hung out on our plat to allow the treacle to drip into a receptacle. But, even after being left for a considerable period of time, a small

---

* Signalling consisted of using flags – two for semaphore and one for Morse. When a competition was held at the end of the session, a boy called Newton Tainsh and I came first equal. At the prize-awarding ceremony, however, only Newton was called to receive the prize. And when I complained to the instructor afterwards, he said that this was due to my behaviour!

111

amount would remain to issue from the holes of the chanter when the pipes were played.

I normally played the mouth organ at any social function, but, when a BB Christmas concert was in the offing, I decided to have a go at singing and learned the words of the 'Lincolnshire Poacher'. This turned out to be a disaster, because there was no rehearsal and the accompanying pianist played in a higher key than I could handle. But, to my own and the audience's embarrassment (especially Eric's), I struggled on to the end.

An officer, dressed as an ARP (Air Raid Precautions) warden, sang 'In my wee gas mask, I'm working out a plan, though all the kids imagine that I'm just a bogey man . . .' – a song of the comedian Dave Willis.

One Saturday afternoon, a few of us hiked to Monikie (our summer camp station), where our young leader said we could spend the night in a shed. Permission to use the shed, however, had not been previously sought. The owner ran a small shop in the village, so we called there to obtain it. Much to our consternation, he refused on the grounds that he had strawberries in the adjacent field and was fearful of us plundering them. Now, if he had allowed us to use his shed and put us on our honour not to touch them, we would have kept our word. But, as it was impossible for us to make the return journey to Dundee that day, we used his shed anyway and had a few of his berries. It was a small shed, there were about seven of us and, packed like herrings in a barrel, we spent an extremely hot and uncomfortable night.

My leisure time was not entirely devoted to the Boys' Brigade, and there was the inevitable increasing interest in the opposite sex. The great meeting place was 'the dancing', and I must have been only fifteen when I became a regular patron of Robertson's West End Palais in the Well Road, immediately off the Hawkhill, in an area now occupied by the University of Dundee.

Robertson's, or Robbie's as it was familiarly called, was run by the small and slightly built Mr Robertson, who had been a ballroom champion and who impressed us greatly by informing us that he had met the band-leader and ballroom dancing expert Victor Silvester.* We beginners went to Robertson's on Saturday afternoons, and this became the highlight of the week. My pal, John Noble, who also worked in Henry's, lived in a tenement at the corner of Wilkies' Lane and Hawkhill, and I can still picture his mother waving to us as we two young bloods – me carrying my glassy kid dancing shoes – headed down the Well Road towards Robbie's. John's father was never there. While serving with the Highland Division, he had been captured at St Valéry, during the Dunkirk evacuation in 1940, and was a prisoner of war in Poland.

---

* After seeing Victor Silvester being interviewed on television, in January 1978, I wrote to him and received a pleasant reply. I was particularly glad that I wrote as he collapsed and died, at the age of seventy-eight, on a beach near Nice, just over six months later.

Robertson's was an excellent venue for youngsters. We paid only 1s 6d (7½p) for admission. Having changed into our dancing shoes, we presented ourselves on the floor for instruction. Mr Robertson was not merely interested in making a profit, but in promoting ballroom dancing. He lined up all the girls and instructed them in the steps of a particular dance, for example the foxtrot, and then lined up the boys and put us through our paces. The instruction was short, but very good. We paid careful attention, and, after the instruction, danced to records of Victor Silvester and His Strict Tempo Dance Orchestra. I met Barbara at Robertson's, and, in spite of my inherent shyness, arranged to meet her inside Kidd's Ballroom in Lindsay Street on a Saturday evening. This was the 'big-time'. The meeting was illicit in that my parents were not told. Barbara paid her own way in, but I bought her a lemonade and, after the dance, escorted her to the East Station, where she caught the train to Monifieth.

The real 'big-time' was The Palais (de Dance) in Tay Street, which is long defunct although the building still stands. Eventually almost all the young people entered its portals, and I remember the Palais with particular affection. It was a lovely ballroom where we danced to the first-class music of Andy Lothian and His Band, although Andy himself was serving somewhere in the Middle East. After paying our entrance money, we passed an elderly gentleman who sat at a table at the end of a corridor and who always wished us a pleasant evening. That was all that gentleman did, and today he would be considered to have performed a totally uneconomic function. But I appreciated his interest and remember him as an integral part of the Palais.

Although there were other dance halls, such as the Locarno in Lochee Road, the Princess at the docks and the Chalet in Broughty Ferry, the Palais was the centre of life for the majority of young Dundonians and even for many from outlying areas. More than a dance hall, it was a place where young people could gather and many of us met our future spouses there. It was incumbent upon a young man to ask a girl to dance. He could approach an unknown girl when such an approach would be considered offensive elsewhere. Only soft drinks were sold in dance halls in these days, and the 'boozers' came in when the pubs closed at 9.30 p.m. On occasion, some entered the worse for wear, but these were the exception and most people had no interest in alcohol.

Many of the young people in the office were also interested in going to private dances. These dances were usually held in Kidd's Rooms, and someone would get us tickets to the annual dance of, say, jute industries or the police. The small group who came from Broughty Ferry were particularly active, and, on at least two occasions, I attended functions in Jolly's Tavern in Broughty Ferry. One of these was a fancy dress ball which the group organised, and costumes were supplied by Douglas Cunningham, a member of the local amateur dramatic society. I went as Sir Walter Raleigh, with stockings given to me by my mother. On my way into the city centre, I was whistling on the top deck of a tram when a man told me to 'give it a rest'. I wondered what he would have said if he had known what I was wearing under my raincoat!

Another function which I attended in Jolly's, once a meeting place of men of the whaling fleet, was the twenty-first birthday party of Anna Oswald, a friend of Joyce Gamble who worked in the office. Because we would miss the last tram back to Dundee, three of us cycled to Broughty Ferry. I was wearing my kilt and was invited to sit beside the birthday girl at the top table. This was another piece of information withheld from my parents, but John gleefully conveyed it to them so that they could rib me about it!

All places of entertainment were closed on Sundays, but I overcame this by joining the St Andrews Film Society, which showed foreign and educational films on Sunday evenings in the La Scala cinema in the Murraygate. Everyone had a gas mask, although these were not generally carried. However, you were denied entrance to a cinema if you didn't have it with you.

Many of the office staff, both men and women, did voluntary night duty at the Eastern Report Centre of the ARP, and, as young men and women were called-up to the forces, the younger ones were asked to fill their places. Pat Tully invited me to join during 1942. I was eager to do so and looked upon this as an honour.

Dundee's Eastern Report Centre was in Victoria Road Primary School, situated almost across the road from Henry's building. I went every Friday night, and each night began with an exercise when we went through what we would have to do if bombs fell in our area. We were the centre controlling fire, ambulance and other services required during an air raid. The exercise lasted about an hour. After this, we got down to the serious business of enjoying ourselves.

The two main activities were table tennis and billiards (on a small, portable table). When the girls and older folks (anyone over about twenty-five) wanted to get into their camp beds in what was by daytime a classroom, we young lads retired to the lavatory where we played pontoon (for pennies) far into the night. The men and women slept in what was really one big room divided by a partition which did not go fully up to the ceiling. Sometimes we indulged in high jinks, and there was at least one night when a pair of trousers was thrown over the partition into the women's section. This equally amused the girls of our own age, but brought reproof from others who were trying to sleep.

A lady came in to cook breakfast for us on the Saturday morning, and I was always exhausted for the rest of the day. The whole business was most enjoyable and the subsistence payment of five shillings (twenty-five pence) was double what my mother gave me for pocket money. But, as I drew nearer the age of eighteen, my own call-up was approaching.

20 A Precipitous Entrance into the Merchant Navy

I wondered which service I would join. Perhaps the most glamorous was the Royal Air Force. Had my eyesight been good, I would have chosen the flying option, but as I had worn glasses since the age of four this was out of the question. Because I played the bagpipes in the Boys' Brigade, I gave some thought to becoming a piper in a Highland regiment, when something previously unknown to me was brought to my notice.

I sometimes frequented Johnston's billiard saloon at the bottom of Blackness Avenue, and it was there that I saw young men carrying earphones. I learned that they were attending evening classes at the wireless college in nearby Windsor Street and were training to become radio officers in the Merchant Navy. As the MN was always in the news and 'enjoyed' a glory somewhat similar to that of the RAF, I was unaware that it was not one of the armed forces of the Crown. A seed was sown in my mind, and I began to investigate the possibility of becoming a radio officer. The more I thought of the idea, the more it appealed to me. I learned that, if I could pass an examination after about six months' study at the wireless college, I could not only enter an heroic service but also be an officer into the bargain! After investigation and a great deal of thought, I put the idea to my mother.

My mother was the one to whom any problem could be brought. It was not that my father was unsympathetic as he was the more sentimental, but often he did not grasp the practicalities of a problem. I half expected my mother to disapprove and to plead with me not to consider proceeding on such a dangerous course. Maybe I hoped that she would. But, much to my surprise, she accepted the idea without the anticipated hysteria and said only that I must consult my father. And it was with trepidation that I did.

My father had been strongly patriotic during the First World War and enlisted at the age of seventeen. But he had survived to learn that the Promised Land 'fit for heroes to live in' did not materialize as he and millions of others joined the ranks of the unemployed during the 1920s and 1930s. Strangely enough, he did not oppose my idea of joining the Merchant Navy, but his immediate reaction surprised me as he said that many young lads like myself thought it would be great to visit foreign countries without thinking about the danger of being at sea. This justified my assessment of my father as I had considered only what it was like at sea, while the pleasure of visiting other countries had never entered my head. He then said that I could attend evening classes at the wireless college, but I immediately opposed this idea as I was then seventeen and a half and had to enter the Merchant Service before I was called-up at the age of eighteen. He accepted my argument and agreed that I should become a full-time student at the college. This was a major economic decision. The cost of full-time tuition for six months was £20 plus an additional £1 to sit the examination – a considerable sum for my parents. In addition, there was the loss of my 'salary'.

I was to reach the call-up age of eighteen towards the end of April 1943, so in November 1942 I informed my employer that I wished to leave at the end of the year in order to attend the wireless college. Mr Archbold, the company secretary, asked me to postpone my entrance to the college until the middle of January. He was a nice man, but he considered only the interests of the company. Because of his charm, I agreed to his request although this reduced the time I would have at the college. Nevertheless, I felt pleasure in being asked to postpone my departure as this was a recognition of my importance.

When I eventually left A. & S. Henry & Co., I was rewarded with a month's salary although I had worked only a fortnight. This was indeed a magnanimous gesture. I was given something like three pounds when entitled to only thirty shillings (£1.50).

The period of five and a half months which I spent at Dundee wireless college was a happy one. I was no longer a pupil working because I was told to do so, but a student with an objective. When at school, I had never had an objective and had been a 'dreamer' and a mediocre scholar. Now I became aware that I was one of the best in my class.

The Elliot McIntosh Wireless College, housed in a former mansion which stood in its own grounds, was a very busy place. There were two classes of private fee-paying students with about ten to fifteen students in each class. Almost all of these were boys of sixteen and seventeen who wished enter the Merchant Navy. But one student was interested in entering the 'Y' service,* and there were four girls, at least two of whom were hoping for employment with the BBC. One class was three months in advance of the other.

Most students were from middle class homes and had been to 'better' schools than Logie Central. But the college was filled to capacity with Royal Navy personnel – men and women training to be telegraphists. Many of these were billeted in Mather's Hotel (renamed the Tay Hotel sometime after the war), near the Taybridge Station, and marched to and from the college. The private (civilian) students were very much in the minority.

My course of study was towards the Postmaster General's Special Certificate in Radiotelegraphy. During peacetime, holders of this certificate could be radio operators on trawlers or other small vessels only, but, during the war, they could be 3rd or 2nd radio officers on merchant ships. In order to qualify for the 'Special', we had to be able to send and receive Morse at twenty words a minute, demonstrate our ability to operate marine radio equipment and answer questions on wireless theory and the regulations applying to radio

---

* A service that monitored all foreign transmissions in the Morse code.

communications to the satisfaction of a GPO examiner. There was no written examination. The Merchant Navy needed radio officers in a hurry, and this was how it was done. The 'wastage' at sea was considerable, but there was never a shortage of young recruits. Although I had believed that there were no women radio officers, this proved not to be the case as a few Norwegians, one Canadian and one Brit were already at sea.

Our days at the wireless college were taken up with learning and then improving our Morse, studying the theory of wireless and the practicalities of the job we were preparing to enter. The Morse room consisted of a number of tables fitted with Morse keys and sockets into which we plugged our earphones. A great deal of time was spent sending Morse to one another, using mainly newspapers to provide the content of the messages. Sometimes we took down Morse sent by an instructor, and it was our constant endeavour to be able to receive and send at yet faster and faster speeds. Learning Morse is a grind which can be compared with learning to touch-type. Once the keyboard is mastered, it needs sheer practice and perseverance. There is no short cut. We constantly missed letters and whole words as we were always trying to receive at speeds too fast for us. This is the only way to improve and at times it seems so disheartening. You think you will never do it. Then suddenly you notice the improvement, and you move from five to ten words a minute.

We had a break from studies every morning at about

10.45 a.m. It is with some amusement that I recall that every morning during our break a van arrived with buns for the RN personnel. We lined the passage as the buns were carried into the building on bakers' trays and, as the trays passed us, our hands went out and we 'nicked' our requirements. Courtesy of the Royal Navy, I had three buns every morning. We were lectured on our behaviour and the buns were then put into a storeroom before we were released for our break. The storeroom was an outside room with bars on the windows, but we could get our arms between the bars and still had our ration. I know the budding RN telegraphists would have done the same.

The obvious answers were either to provide a few extra buns for those entering the sister service or allow the RN to have first break. But these solutions were never found by those in charge. I enjoyed free buns until the end of my time at the college and enjoyed them all the more because of the sport we had in obtaining them.

During my time at the wireless college, I continued to spend my Friday nights on duty at the Eastern Report Centre – which was just as well as this provided me with pocket money. In the autumn of 1942, I had as usual enrolled for evening classes at Logie and, although it now seems ludicrous that I did so, I continued to attend the classes while at wireless college and succeeded in passing the exams. Eventually, in June, the diet of tests towards the Special Certificate arrived, and I found myself qualified to become a radio officer. I had never before experienced such a successful academic year and, because the staffing situation at sea had improved, I looked forward to some weeks of leisure before going to sea.

Some two or three months previously, I had received notification of my impending call-up into the Armed Forces and had undergone a medical examination in the Maryatt Hall, within the Caird Hall building. As I wore spectacles, I knew that my eyesight was not perfect, but otherwise believed myself to be fit. I do, however, have a malformation of the chest, and, because of this, the doctor who examined me called upon a colleague for a second opinion. This doctor was an older man and he too found nothing wrong but, to be on the safe side, I was graded A2 rather than the A1 which would have signified that I was in first class condition. I remember the older doctor trying to reassure me by saying that he had a friend who had lived till sixty with the same malformation, and I equally remember not being at all impressed by this and saying, 'What? Only to sixty?'

After the medical examination, there was an intelligence test which dealt entirely with shapes. The test was graded in difficulty, so that the problems became more difficult as I proceeded. I have no idea of the result, but imagine I had everything right up to the point where I began to experience difficulty and when the time limit expired. I have always been careful, neat and methodical and, consequently, somewhat slow. I still have no idea of my IQ and appreciate my ignorance of it. I have always suspected that it is not all that high, but, if this is the case and I had learned of it earlier in life, the knowledge may have inhibited me from tackling what would then have appeared to be insurmountable courses of study in the future.

There was also an interview with a retired Army colonel who wanted to know which service I wished to join. My reply was 'The Merchant Navy'. This answer, of course, he was not allowed to accept and so he explained that I had to choose one of the Armed Forces of the Crown: the Army, Royal Navy or Royal Air Force. The fact that there were guns on merchant ships and that merchant seamen were firing these guns did not make the Merchant Navy one of the 'Armed Forces'. I appreciated the colonel's position and knew that he appreciated mine. Perhaps he wrote Royal Navy on the form relating to me, but I do not know.

Also, during my time at the college, I was called before a tribunal as I had applied for a postponement of call-up in order to enter the Merchant Navy. My father attended the tribunal with me, and it consisted of three men. The chairman, a well-known Dundee solicitor, was very antagonistic towards me and made it clear that he considered that I was 'dodging the column'. Unfortunately for him, one of his colleagues on the board was an employer whose son had trained at a civilian fee-paying establishment before flying with the RAF. This man took great exception to the chairman's remarks, and, as the other man must have agreed with him, I was given the time to complete my course, providing I passed the June examination. (And it was only later that I learned that the antagonistic chairman's son had indeed evaded the call-up by embarking on an engineering apprenticeship at the late age of seventeen.)

The majority of radio officers were employed by the Marconi Company, Siemens and International Marine Radio, which were wireless companies supplying both men and equipment to the shipping lines. Long before I became interested in the sea, however, I had heard my father, an engineering fitter in the Caledon shipyard, extolling the virtues of the ships they built for Alfred Holt & Co. of Liverpool, who owned the Blue Funnel Line and the Glen Line. And, as Holt employed their men direct, I applied to them as soon as I qualified.

I had expected a few weeks' holiday between passing the Special Certificate in Radiotelegraphy and going to sea, but this proved woefully inaccurate. I collected my certificate at the wireless college on the afternoon of 30 June 1943 and was still in bed the following morning when a telegram arrived calling me for interview at Holt's office at 9 a.m. the following day. It is one thing preparing to enter an heroic service and basking in its limelight, but quite another thing going. But, like thousands of others, I was caught in the tide of events and, within two hours of receiving that telegram, boarded a crowded train for Liverpool.

After two days of interviews and a medical examination, I was told to return home, get myself kitted out and report at the dock gate at Greenock on the morning of 7 July with my luggage marked with the letter M. I arrived back in Dundee on the morning of Sunday the 4th, so I had only Monday and part of Tuesday to get ready.

My mother accompanied me to the Mercantile Marine office in Dock Street, where I joined the Merchant Navy and was given my seaman's identity card and my Continuous Certificate of Discharge – the latter between thin, light blue, wartime cardboard covers and bearing the embossed stamp of the Ministry of War Transport. I was also given the silver MN lapel badge, the only 'uniform' of MN ratings. My mother also came with me to buy my uniform, at the large main shop of Dundee Eastern Cooperative Society in the Seagate, as well as the bare minimum of the clothes which did not include white tropical uniform as we thought only of the North Atlantic. By Tuesday evening, I was ready and, wearing my new uniform with its one wavy gold band, said goodbye to my grandparents in their house on the landing below and lastly to Mother and Eric.

My father went with me on the train to Glasgow, where we found it almost impossible to find overnight accommodation, and ended up on chairs and a settee in the sitting room of a guest house. While looking for a place to stay, we were in the foyer of an hotel with a group of men in civilian clothes whom we took to be Merchant Navy officers, and I was to learn that even during the war few senior MN officers ever wore uniform ashore, as this had not been their custom in peacetime. That same evening, when we visited a public toilet, a drunk man staggered on to a weighing machine and asked me to read his weight. I had little experience of drunk men, and the incident emphasised the fact that I was entering a very different world.

On the morning of Wednesday, 7 July, we took the train to Greenock, and when we arrived at the dock gate, the place seemed deserted. There was little sign of traffic and, apart from the policeman on duty at the gate, there was nobody about. On showing my pass to the policeman, I was directed to a large shed at some distance from the dock gate. As my father was not allowed into the dock area, I said to him that I would probably be able to come out again once I had reported myself present, and set off down that lonely dock road carrying my one suitcase and feeling awkward in my brand-new uniform covered by the standard dark blue Merchant Navy raincoat. I didn't look back. I had a pretty shrewd idea that I would not be allowed to return to the dock gate, but felt that this was an easier way to say farewell. My assumption proved correct. My father waited at the gate for two hours before beginning his journey back to Dundee, and I didn't see him, or Dundee, again until Thursday, 19 October, 1944.